Wimbledon the 16
R Zeigler of July
[1800]

Beautiful flower Bas-
itely obliged to you, I
say'd on these occasions
r little mind attention;
to hear Lord Lansdown
shou'd recover invalids
y the better for it which
as are to hear, I hope Miss
er Rheumatism, it was
to be lay'd up upon going
eseemes so fond of, I sa
rning before he went a

ARISTOCRATS

THE ILLUSTRATED COMPANION TO THE TELEVISION SERIES

ARISTOCRATS

THE ILLUSTRATED COMPANION TO THE TELEVISION SERIES

Stella Tillyard

WEIDENFELD & NICOLSON

LONDON

CONTENTS

FRONTISPIECE
Lady Sarah Lennox aged about fifteen, saucily plump in pearl choker, deep ruffles and black lace mantilla, painted by Francis Coates during her first London season.
BACKGROUND RIGHT
The Lennox family home, Goodwood in Sussex, as it looked at the end of the eighteenth century.

Dramatis Personae

CHARLES LENNOX, 2ND DUKE OF RICHMOND (1701–50)

The careful son of a feckless father and grandson of Charles II, the 2nd Duke of Richmond's life was dedicated to establishing the family's probity after a rocky start. Married against his wishes as a teenager to Sarah Cadogan (1703–51), he left his bride in the nursery while he travelled round Europe, coming back three years later to find her a beautiful woman. They produced seven children during their happy marriage and the Duke went on to become a model courtier and Master of the Horse to George II. He died of a fever in 1750 and the Duchess died a year later, leaving three little girls to be brought up by their older daughter Emily in Ireland.

Richmond is played in the series by Julian Fellowes, Sarah his wife by Diane Fletcher.

CAROLINE LENNOX (1723–74)

Richmond's eldest child, Caroline was an intense, anxious and intelligent girl, fascinated by moral questions and strongly attracted to people and ideas considered dangerous by her conventional parents. Refusing all their carefully vetted aristocratic suitors, she fell in love at the age of 20 with Henry Fox, a fat, ambitious, greedy and licentious politician 18 years her senior. Disregarding the horror of her parents and modelling herself on the heroines of the 'story books' she was so fond of reading, Caroline eloped with Henry in 1744. Their marriage was blissfully happy. Caroline's life was dedicated to her husband, her three sons, her sisters and her love of learning. She remained a voracious reader, bilingual – like her siblings – in French and English. An admirer of the French *philosophes* and a lover of Roman history, she spent a good deal of time in Paris and travelled to Italy in 1766 to see the places she had read about in ancient history. Profoundly pessimistic about human nature and always expecting the worst, it eventually came: Henry suffered a series of strokes in the early 1770s and she got cancer. They died within a month of each other in 1774.

Caroline is played in the series by Serena Gordon.

HENRY FOX, 1ST LORD HOLLAND (1705–74)

Son of a prominent court servant to Charles II who died when he was young, Henry had to make his own fortune and way in the world. A brilliant and unscrupulous man, loyal to the family but little else, he shocked acquaintances with his atheism, but won them over with his charm. Initially a Tory, he changed sides when it became obvious after the Hanoverian Succession that the Tories were out of favour, used his connections to find himself a Parliamentary seat and joined Walpole's government. He rose to become Minister at War and Paymaster of the Forces, making a huge fortune during the Seven Years War. Accused of negotiating a disadvantageous peace and vilified for making a fortune from public funds, he retired under a cloud in 1765, disappointed at having failed to secure the one office he really wanted: that of Prime Minister. The love of his family was not henceforth enough to sustain him, and he died, from boredom as much as old age, in 1774.

Henry is played in the series by Alun Armstrong.

STE FOX, 2ND LORD HOLLAND (1747–75), CHARLES JAMES FOX (1749–1806)
AND SUSAN FOX-STRANGWAYS (1743–1827)

Caroline and Henry's oldest son Ste, afflicted from babyhood by shaking and fits, was his mother's favourite.
Debilitated by years of taking heavy metals and other poisons for his ailments, he grew to be fat, amiable and deaf.
He married Mary Fitzpatrick, fathered a son and survived his parents by less than a year.

Charles James Fox was the most famous Opposition politician of the century and arguably its most famous face,
painted, sculpted and, especially, drawn in cartoons, more than any other. Tolerant, easy-going and with his father's
charm, he was as his friend Edmund Burke said, 'a man made to be loved'. Caroline hoped that he would become
Lord Chancellor, but he spurned the law for politics, earning the soubriquet 'Champion of the People' for
his promotion of civil rights, his unceasing hostility to the monarch George III and his insistence on
the sovereignty of Parliament. An unreformed libertine and bon viveur, he married a courtesan,
Elizabeth Armistead, and spurned a title on his death-bed in 1806.

Susan Fox-Strangways was Henry Fox's niece. An intelligent, angry girl, she became Sarah Lennox's confidante
when the latter arrived from Ireland in 1759 and remained her friend and correspondent for the rest of her life.
Susan shocked her family by eloping in 1764 with a matinée idol William O'Brien. After a brief sojourn in
New York, they settled in the West Country and lived an unremarkable country life.

Ste Fox is played by Toby Jones and Charles James Fox is played by Hugh Sachs. Susan Fox-Strangways is played by Pauline McLynn.

EMILY LENNOX (1731–1814)

Emily was her parents' favourite, a beautiful grey-blue-eyed, auburn-haired child who felt entitled to, and generally got, everything she wanted. For 18 years after her marriage to the Earl of Kildare, Emily lived an adored, expensive and pampered life, the mistress of two of the grandest houses in Ireland and mother of a huge family. But in 1765, her eldest son died, and another side of her personality came to the fore. Beneath her demanding nature she was obsessive, anxious and looking for a passionate relationship. She found it with a Scottish schoolmaster, William Ogilvie, tutor to her children, and when her husband died in 1773, Emily stunned her family and scandalized Dublin society by marrying Ogilvie. They lived in France for several years before returning to Ireland, and, eventually settling in London. Emily had three more children in France, bringing her total to 22, of whom 12 lived to maturity.

Emily is played in the series by
Hayley Griffiths, Geraldine Somerville and Sian Phillips.

JAMES FITZGERALD, EARL OF KILDARE AND DUKE OF LEINSTER (1722–73)

Kildare inherited his earldom at an early age, and with it the position of head of Ireland's aristocracy. Confined to political opposition by virtue of his own hostility to English influence in Ireland, and by long family tradition, Kildare contented himself with living grandly, producing a large family and making life difficult for a series of Lords Lieutenant. Deeply in love with his wife, his passion was returned only as fondness, and his children grew to fear him and find him a distant figure.

Kildare is played in the series by Ben Daniels.

WILLIAM OGILVIE (1740–1832)

Emily's second husband, William Ogilvie took the place of their father in the lives of the younger Fitzgeralds as well as in their mother's affections. A tall, dour, ugly man, he was yet extremely attractive to many women. He was the only person in Emily's life who was able to win her submission and she adored him for it, remaining passionately entangled with him for several decades after they fell in love. A tough man physically and emotionally, Ogilvie lived to grow rich and extremely old, never completely accepted in polite society, but living life on his own terms, uncompromisingly.

William Ogilvie is played in the series by George Anton and David Gant.

LORD EDWARD FITZGERALD (1763–98)

Edward was Emily's favourite son and Ogilvie's favourite pupil. A soldier as a young man, Lord Edward made contact with the radical United Irishmen when he returned with his French wife Pamela from revolutionary Paris in 1792. When the United Irishmen went underground so did he, ending up as the *de facto* commander of the ill-fated Irish rebellion of 1798. Betrayed by an informer he was arrested, thrown in gaol and died of septicaemia the day before the rebellion broke out.

Lord Edward is played in the series by Andrew Fitzsimmons and John Light, Pamela his wife by Virginie Astor.

Tom Conolly (1738–1803)

Tom Conolly was married to Louisa Lennox because he was the wealthiest commoner in Ireland, the Earl of Kildare's closest neighbour and a political follower as well. He was an amiable, stupid man, who loved his wife and his horses in equal measure. Politically he moved with the times, beginning as something of a liberal and in opposition to Dublin Castle, ending up on the Castle side, although he remained opposed to Ireland's union with Britain.

Tom Conolly is played by Tom Mullion and Paul Ridley.

Louisa Conolly (1743–1821)

Louisa was the third of the Lennox sisters, and the one with the least turbulent life. Brought up in Ireland, she was married at 15 to Ireland's richest man, Tom Conolly. To her great sadness she remained childless, living her life as a pattern of goodness to which less virtuous members of the family, especially Sarah, aspired. For six decades she devoted herself to her sisters, their children, her husband and her great mansion of Castletown.

Louisa is played in the series by Saoirse O'Brien, Anne-Marie Duff and Diana Quick.

Sarah Lennox (1745–1826)

After a disastrous flirtation with the young George III, Sarah was married at 17 to Sir Charles Bunbury, a Suffolk baronet. The sexiest and least secure of the Lennox sisters, she paid a heavy price for the interest the monarch had shown in her. Her marriage was a disaster and she embarked on a series of affairs, which culminated in her having an illegitimate child by Lord William Gordon (above) and leaving her husband to live with him. Persuaded out of that liaison by her family, she endured more than a decade of lonely ostracism on her brother's Goodwood estate before marrying George Napier, a handsome career soldier several years her junior. From then on her fortunes improved. She and Napier moved to Ireland, where they lived close to Louisa in Celbridge, County Kildare. Sarah finally found happiness and founded a dynasty of soldiers, dying in 1826 famous both for having nearly become Queen of England and for being the mother of famous men.

Sarah is played in the series by Lara Madden, Jodhi May and Sheila Ruskin.
Charles Bunbury and Lord William Gordon are played by Andrew Havill and Gary Cady.

COLONEL GEORGE NAPIER (1751–1804)

Six foot tall and described as 'the most perfect made man in the
British army', George Napier was already married when he fell in
love with Sarah Lennox when he was serving in her brother's
regiment and she was living on the Goodwood estate. Sent to
America in 1779 to avoid attaching yet another scandal to Sarah's
name, he conveniently lost his wife and two children to yellow fever
in New York, which enabled him to return a widower in 1781 and
claim Sarah's hand. The marriage was an exceptionally happy one,
although Napier himself was an unsuccessful soldier,
and died of cancer at the age of 53.

George Napier is played in the series by Martin Glyn Murray and Jeremy Bulloch.

Charles Lennox, 3rd Duke of Richmond (1735–1806)

An intelligent, pedantic man, he never achieved the political prominence his intellect deserved, having no talent for intrigue or attracting followers. He was unloved by his sisters Caroline and Emily, adored by Louisa and intermittently loved and hated by Sarah, whom he protected after her disastrous affair with William Gordon and then alienated by his insistence upon his prerogative as head of the family to be able to decide her fate. For the last two decades of the century he served in William Pitt's government as Master of the Ordnance, but his political life was dominated by his rivalry with his nephew Charles James Fox, and his family relations by his unsuccessful attempt to get his sisters Emily and Sarah to support his political position. He married Mary Bruce, and although he was the father of three illegitimate daughters, the marriage did not produce an heir, which perhaps contributed to the Duchess's bitterness in later life.

The 3rd Duke is played in the series by William Sparks and Tom Beard and his wife Mary by Katherine Wogan.

THE ROYAL FAMILY

George II is played in the series by *Clive Swift*,

and his grandson the Prince of Wales,

who became George III in 1760,

by *Luke de Lacy*.

Introduction

TWELVE GLOBULAR WHITE PAPER lanterns hang on improvised wires from the magnificent plaster and gilt ceiling. Ragged square pieces of black-out cloth lie on top, stopping the light filtering upwards and making the lamps look like Christmas puddings with the colour reversed. Electric cables, bundled together, wind dangerously across the mahogany floor, and run like jungle creepers up walls and pillars. In the middle of the huge room soundmen hang on ladders and, at arms' length, raise and lower thin booms with microphones attached to them, as if they were fishing in the sky. Below them stand several carefully composed groups of extras. Their foot positions are marked by the clapper loader, a man who moves swiftly about carrying rolls of coloured masking tape like coloured bagels on a looped string, and, biting lengths off with his teeth, makes angles on the wooden floor on which the actors can place and replace their feet during rehearsals and innumerable takes.

It is a bright and chilly autumn day outside, but the room is artificially lit, muggy and slightly claustrophic despite its size. The long windows facing the garden and all the doors are sealed with black-out cloth and the atmosphere within is thickened with a pearly mist shot from a machine like a squat cannon. An oily milkiness covers everyone — soundmen, electricians, the camera crew, the quiet director and his tensely energetic assistant clutching a walkie-talkie, make-up artists, props men, costume people, script prompters, the stills photographer, actors, extras and bystanders — and gives the whole scene a lush and distant sombreness.

We are in the great salon of Carton House in County Kildare, Ireland. An assembly is in full swing. Its host is William Fitzgerald, 2nd Duke of Leinster; the year is about 1795. Little knots of people move about miming chatter. They walk singly and in couples back and forth across the path of the camera like shuttles weaving a piece of cloth until the tapestry of the scene is choreographed, rehearsed and ready for shooting. Everyone is richly dressed in evening wear; plum red and dusky purple frock coats, silk gowns of bottle green or maroon shot with black, stiff and rustling like tissue paper. Pearl chokers, lace ruffles, crisp cravats and silver shoe buckles stand out hazily in the milky light. On a gold and ormolu sofa at the end of the room, two actors are talking quietly: Sian Phillips, magnificent in powder blue, playing Emily, Duchess of Leinster, and David Gant, who is playing her second husband, William Ogilvie. Earlier he, too, has been rehearsing, standing as William Ogilvie stands in the only known sketch of him, thin and stork-like, with his shoulders hunched and his face to the floor, chewing his lips. Above the golden sofa on the end wall of the salon, is Emily herself, painted by Allan Ramsay in 1765, reading a large folio volume and seated at an occasional table. Looking from the actors to the original, I feel more than a little uneasy, wondering what she would have made of the proceedings beneath her.

In death we have no privacy. As soon as we fall silent,

others can start talking, writing and filming; there is no law to protect us. As writers we try to make our pictures full and rounded, but they are necessarily partial and shaped by our own times. In the end we write and dramatize other lives for our own entertainment and edification, and with our own motives. Certain subjects – and perhaps Emily was one of them – want history to justify their own conduct, and the times have certainly come to her defence. In her own time she would have been condemned for her love affair with William Ogilvie and her clandestine second marriage. But now she could look down on the bustle beneath her and see that she has become the heroine of a great and extravagant drama; one that, with her taste for excess she might even, as her sister Caroline would have put it, 'have enjoyed vastly'.

Emily, it is true, more than half deliberately left her secrets to be discovered by future generations. But would her sisters have wanted their triumphs and their follies placed between covers and then put on the screen? Caroline, we can be sure, would not. In her letters she was the most open of the Lennox sisters, sharing, especially with Emily, her moments of happines and her complicated hopes and worries. But she would never have countenanced them going beyond her family circle; she had a fear

of 'the mob', as she called ordinary people, and the idea of them – us – reading and watching her life story would have impossible and unpardonable. Louisa? She was in many ways the most private of the sisters, and ordered the destruction of her papers after her death, determined to leave behind a legacy of goodness and nothing else. But she was a lover of poular entertainment and had a secret interest in dressing up and concealment. Perhaps, suitably disguised and discreetly hidden, she might have enjoyed watching herself in her customary supporting role. As for Sarah, she was a natural actress and would surely have seized the most histrionic and dramatic part – her own.

To accompany the many paintings and stills here reproduced for the first time, I have written a completely new text, in which I have brought together much unused material from the sisters' letters. I have not written their story chronologically. That was done in the original text of *Aristocrats* – upon which the television series is based – and is done again, in a slightly modified form, in the television drama. Instead I have concentrated on the innumerable details of their lives in country and in town that I could not use the first time around and which are told in in the sisters' own intelligent and witty voices.

Four sisters, four actresses: Caroline – Serena Gordon – stands back left, with Louisa – Anne-Marie Duff – next to her. In front, Sarah – Jodhi May – with Emily – Geraldine Somerville – to the right.

Chapter 1

Beginnings and Marriages

RIGHT

Louise Renée de Kéroualle, Duchess of Portsmouth and Aubigny, painted in her youth by Henri Gascar, 1675. A luscious flower, as this portrait indicates, she was unhesitatingly plucked by Charles II to be his mistress when she arrived in London as a spy from the Court of Louis XIV in 1670, and together they founded the Richmond dynasty.

I**T WASN'T A RESPECTABLE** beginning for a dynasty, but it was certainly grandiose enough: the 1st Duke of Richmond's father was the King of England, his mother a French aristocrat. That she was a spy in the service of Louis XIV – or at the very least a diplomat – and he an adulterous philanderer mattered little; indeed in time it would add to the family's glamour. Sent over from France in 1670 with the Duchess of Orléans to negotiate the secret Treaty of Dover, Louise de Kéroualle immediately caught the roving eye of Charles II, and after the Duchess's death Louis XIV gave her the task of using her sultry beauty to bind the King of England to the French interest and to bring him to Catholicism. In the first she succeeded. The Treaty was signed and war declared against the Protestant Dutch in 1672. The second she never quite managed, Charles prudently maintaining an outward show of Anglican Protestantism until the very end.

Louise did, however, permanently capture the affections of the King, using what the diarist John Evelyn censoriously called her 'childish, simple and baby face' and her other charms with great skill. 'She studied to please and observe' the King 'in everything', wrote Bishop Burnet, another shocked observer of court manners, 'so that he passed away the rest of his life in a great fondness for her. He kept her at a vast charge; and she by many fits of sickness (some believed real and others thought only pretended) gained of him everything she desired.'

Louise was in fact a formidable business woman who, besides securing a handsome

ABOVE

Charles II, by Sir Peter Lely. Although the 'merry monarch' had several long-term mistresses, his devotion to Louise de Kéroualle was genuine. 'I have always loved her, and I die loving her', he declared on his death-bed. After Charles II's death, Louise retired to her château of Aubigny in France and brought up their son, the 1st Duke of Richmond as a Catholic and a Frenchman.

annuity and the title Duchess of Portsmouth from Charles II, and being given two châteaux and a large estate by a grateful Louis XIV, made sure that her son by the King, born in 1672 and christened Charles Lennox, was given a decent clothing of titles and a fine feather bed of income. He was created during his infancy Duke of Richmond, Baron of Settrington and Earl of March in the English peerage, and Baron Methuen of Tarbolton, Earl of Darnley and Duke of Lennox in the Scottish peerage, a useful array of titles which had recently passed back to Charles on the death of the last of his Scottish Stuart relatives. Much more tangibly tradeable, though, was the income the King added: £2,000 a year and a royalty on coal dues at the northern port of Newcastle. It was the latter that was to make the Richmond family fortune. As manufacturing increased, so did their income; a hundred years later the first Duke's grandson

would be one of the wealthiest men in Britain.

The 1st Duke inherited a good deal of his father's charm and some of his mother's shrewdness. Brought up in France after Charles II's death in 1685, he eked out a living as a soldier in Louis XIV's army until he realized that, with a judicious religious shift, he could claim not only his British titles but also his English income. In 1692 he secretly left France, and, arriving in London by way of Switzerland and Germany, was received into the Church of England and the Court of William and Mary. His titles and income were restored soon afterwards and Richmond was henceforth an Anglican, a Whig and a supporter not only of the Glorious Revolution but also of the Hanoverian Succession which brought George I to the throne in 1714. His life, however, was not distinguished by many acts of similar calculation. Before dissipation overcame him, he managed to marry Anne Brudenall, produce the obligatory heir and two daughters, and to buy the estate of Goodwood near Chichester in Sussex in 1697. He succeeded in little else. When not hunting on the south coast, he gambled away his coal money in London, in Paris and anywhere else on the Continent where idle British officers were encamped during the long wars against Louis XIV. In The Hague in 1719, accompanied by his son and heir Charles, Earl of March, Richmond racked up a debt to the Earl of Cadogan, one of Marlborough's staff officers, that was way beyond his severely compromised means. By way of settlement, Richmond unblushingly offered his son as a husband for Cadogan's daughter Sarah and the Earl accepted with equal insouciance, driving the bargain home with the insistence that Sarah's fortune be reduced by a substantial sum as well.

The young couple were far less cheerful about this neat arrangement than their fathers. One story relates that Sarah just stared at her future husband when brought out of the nursery for the marriage ceremony, while he, gazing with the sophistication of 19 at the unprepossessing 13-year-old, burst out in horror, 'Surely they are not going to marry me to that dowdy?' Another maintains that the boy was not even present, being represented only by his cold and mute sword, that lay on a velvet cushion by the bride.

Whatever the case, the young Earl of March

LEFT

Charles Lennox, 2nd Duke of Richmond and his wife Lady Sarah Cadogan, painted by Sir Godfrey Kneller in the 1720s. Married in order to settle a gambling debt between their fathers, the couple met for the first time on their wedding day, when she was thirteen, he nineteen. Indeed, according to one report, he was not even present at his own marriage, his sword lying on a cushion taking his place.

BELOW

Louise de Kéroualle in later life. The grandeur of her apartments in Whitehall, chock-a-block with silver and furniture, prompted the diarist John Evelyn to write censoriously, 'What contentment can there be in the riches and splendours of this world, if purchased with vice and dishonour?'

was in no hurry to assume the married state. He spent three years travelling on the Continent and on his return was dallying in the theatre when he spotted a particularly alluring young woman in a nearby box. Ever his father's son, he enquired who she was. 'You must be a stranger in London', came the reply, 'not to know the toast of the town, the beautiful Lady March.'

It was here in more than the obvious biological sense that the lives of Caroline, Emily,

Louisa and Sarah Lennox began, for their own marriages – and thus, because they were women, the shape of their existences – were to be defined by the unexpected and unusual marital happiness of their parents. In the first place it confirmed to the Duke and Duchess their right to choose partners for their children, as they were chosen for one another. In the second, it encouraged the children to look for and expect a marital felicity beyond the dynastic considerations that formed the core of most aristocratic marriages.

The 2nd Duke of Richmond, determined to lay his father's charming and feckless ghost, became a conscientious courtier and father, and, in an unambitious way, a happy man. An heir, however, was slower to arrive than marital felicity. The Duke and Duchess's first child, Caroline, was born in 1723. Although she was not the required son, her birth augured well for the future of the dynasty, as the Duchess of Portsmouth was quick to point out, congratulating her grandson in a note from France: 'give a thousand kind messages to your wife from me, and tell her, from me, to be very careful of her health, so that next year she may give me a little son! That is what I passionately desire.' The Duchess obliged, but the boy died after a few hours, prompting the implacable Louise to write, 'she has not kept her promise to me, though. For last year she promised me a son, but – dear child – I'm sure she is very sorry to

MADEMOISELLE DE·KEROUALLE ENSVITE DUCHESSE·DE· PORTSMOUTH ET·D'AUBIGNY·

LEFT

George II – Clive Swift – sits back on the throne at an assembly in St James's in about 1759. 'I kissed the King's hand today', wrote the Earl of Kildare to his wife Emily that year. 'He looks just as he did, but less colour, and one eye gone.' A year later the King had a heart attack sitting on his commode after breakfast, and died on the spot.

Lady Emily Lennox, aged about twelve, played by Hayley Griffiths, and her sister Caroline, played by Serena Gordon. Her parents' favourite, Emily was immensely precocious and pretty. 'Em is admirable but horribly naughty', the Duchess wrote when Emily was little. Emily expected to be given exactly what she wanted all her life and generally she was.

have failed in her promise! But I hope that her third will be an increase of the right sort in your family.' It wasn't, but the Duchess went on trying, producing twelve children, of whom seven lived to maturity. Several children were born after Caroline but all until Emily, born in 1731, followed their brother to his early grave. An heir, Charles, who became the 3rd Duke, was finally born in 1735. George, in honour of King George II, in whose household the Duke was by then working, was born in 1737, then Louisa in 1743, Sarah in 1745 and Cecilia in 1750, when her mother was 44.

The 2nd Duke was not merely a good family man; he was also determined to be an exemplary gentleman, in country and town, in the army camp and the library. His life, like that of other very wealthy aristocrats connected to the court,

was lived in the public gaze. In all his activities he was on display; even his most private acts were also public. So mingled were the family and the monarchy, the familial and the ceremonial, the homely and the ostentatious that no distinction between public duty and private pleasure was possible. The public was the private and the private the public. And this was equally true in Court and cricket field, barracks and library.

At Goodwood, which the Lennox family always considered the home to which they all belonged, the Duke could be a family man, shut away in his imposing (but already old-fashioned) Jacobean mansion, surrounded by children, hounds and horses. But he shared the place with servants, stewards, guests, protégés and hangers-on. He was constantly on display and very conscious of acting his part as paterfamilias and local paternalist. Beyond the park gates the Duke mingled with the local people in the Charlton Hunt and in village cricket matches. But these brief forays into the social emulsifier of sport were matched by his duties as Lord Lieutenant of Sussex and High Steward of Chichester, which he held as the biggest local landowner and most elevated local aristocrat. Within the house, the family and the monarchy were equally mixed together. Charles II, grandfather and King, gazed down from the walls. Nearby, Charles I, painted with his wife and children, reminded the family of the dire consequences of failing to understand the temper of the times.

The 2nd Duke needed little prodding. He was punctilious to the letter about his duties at the Hanoverian Court and in the army. At the Court of George II, Richmond had a worthy but unspectacular career. He specialized in managing royal ceremonials, ensuring that the layers of ritual in which majesty lay enfolded remained intact and impenetrable. At the King's coronation in 1727 he performed the office of Lord High Constable, which meant that he was in charge of all the practical arrangements upon which the ceremonial rested. He managed the crowd, the seating arrangements for visiting dignitaries and diplomats, the movement of the procession through the abbey, places for participants to robe, disrobe and relieve themselves. Shortly afterwards he was made a

Lord of the Bedchamber, a post which carried a salary of £500 a year and demanded daily attendance on the monarch when the court was in England. The Duchess held a similar position, at the same salary, with Queen Caroline. Lords and Ladies of the Bedchamber managed the personal needs of the King and Queen. They did very mundane tasks, ordering meals and clothes and rationing visitors; but in

ABOVE

Little Lady Sarah Lennox, aged about five, played by Lara Madden. Highly spirited and something of an actress, she became a favourite with King George II as a little child about the Court, and went on to win the heart of the King's grandson, the future George III.

RIGHT
Racehorses from the 2nd Duke of Richmond's stable exercising on the Sussex Downs, painted about 1760 by the young George Stubbs at the beginning of his career. The 3rd Duke, who commissioned the painting, inherited his father's love of hunting and racing, and established the famous Goodwood Racecourse in 1801, five years before he died.

compensation they were the monarchs' companions and perhaps their friends.

An ambitious courtier, he had constant access to the monarch, saw and perhaps helped to determine who was in and who was out, and he was ideally placed to lobby for a better position. Richmond, however, was anxious not for advancement, but for sobriety and dignity. He stayed on for seven years, the picture of steadiness but not of success. The King called him an affectionate and sincere friend, and in 1737 rewarded him with the Mastership of the Horse, a step up in rank but sideways into the royal stable. There Richmond managed the monarch's movement from palace to palace and from England to the Continent faithfully until his death. It was his job to accompany the retinue wherever it went in England. When George departed for Hanover at the beginning of

the summer, the Duke went as far as Harwich, where he was able to hand the King gratefully over to the Royal Navy and to his Hanoverian counterpart.

Richmond pursued his army career in the Royal Horse Guards, buying his way in as a Captain as soon as he came back from the Grand Tour. He took his duties seriously as he climbed the ladder of command. He fought at Dettingen in 1743, was put in charge of the defence of London during the 1745 rebellion, and ended up at the head of the Regiment. When the Regiment was his, he insisted that it reflect his position and was more than usually careful to make sure that its standards of public display were second to none. 'I have', he wrote, 'seen every man, and every horse; arms, clothing, second mounting, furniture and accoutrements. On Saturday I reviewed the whole regiment together, and a glorious show it made.'

Even for Richmond, however, life was not all courtly business and army protocol. The Duke found ways of, if not abandoning the conventions which encircled his life, then at least changing them. From the constant exposure of aristocratic life, some respite was to be had in dressing up, impersonation and harmless subterfuge. The Duke inherited his father's interest in Freemasonry, he enjoyed practical jokes and he revelled in the theatre.

Freemasonry both aped and subverted the forms of aristocratic life. It was ritualized, hierarchical and exclusive. Like courtiers, Freemasons had special clothes, language and gestures for particular occasions. And like the monarchy, Freemasonry was dependent upon show and had at its heart theatrical mysteries enacted in costume. But whereas at Court the king played the King, at the Masonic lodge Freemasons adopted new secret identities which they carried about with them in the wider world. As a Mason, the Duke was no longer the Duke of Richmond, even though it was incumbent upon him to become Grand Master. He was a Brother, one of a band known only to one

BELOW
Charles, 3rd Duke of Richmond with his brother and Sussex neighbour Lord George Lennox, and members of the Charlton Hunt, also by Stubbs, 1759/60. The Charlton Hunt was established by the 1st Duke and continued enthusiastically by his descendants.

Below

Silk Court gown with very wide hoops from the mid-eighteenth century. Such elaborate outfits were impractical for everyday life and worn only on special occasions, which is one reason why examples survive in such good condition. Ordinary clothes worn by gentlewomen would have been passed to their maids when no longer wanted, and then would have eventually found their way to second-hand warehouses or have been picked apart.

another and he moved invisibly in society recognizable only to his fellows. Such secrecy was appealing to a man whose life was so open to view.

More simple impersonations also had an attraction for the Duke. In 1733, he planned and executed an elaborate highway robbery against a cleric who, he thought, needed to be taken down a peg or two. He arranged for the Reverend Sherwin to travel along the Portsmouth to Petersfield road in the company of the Duchess and their friends Lady Tankerville, Lady Hervey and Mr Henry Fox, all of whom were primed to play their parts to the

hilt. The Duke and a friend hid in a deep ditch, pistols at the ready, until the carriage lumbered by. Then they sprang out and stuck their pistols through the windows. Henry Fox played his part to perfection, first refusing to give way, then taking fright and handing over his money, watch, snuffbox and toothpick case. The ladies followed suit, and after terrifying the Rev. Sherwin by letting off his pistol, the Duke got all his valuables too.

The Duke followed up this triumphant sortie with an account of the joke, written for the amusement of the participants and his friends. In it he created an extraordinary linguistic impersonation of a highwayman, burying his ducal identity in bawdy language and

highwayman's slang, and signing it '+ his marke'. It was inevitably entitled 'Knights of the Road'. The Rev. Sherwin's chastisement was rendered thus: ' "Dam ye,", say I, "your gold and your watch"; upon which he fell a-joking. Slap I lett fly my pop, tho not with the intention to kill the poor dog neither, but the slugs whistled pretty close by his ears, which putt him in a most confounded fright; "take all", says he, upon which I whypt my hand into his pocket, which I could hardly do for his paunch, but at last i lugg'd out his nett, that is his purse, with six shiners and a smelt in it, butt the Dog had no tattle, upon which I cuss'd him as he deserved.'

The Duke soon reassumed his public position as a good citizen, model of filial piety and tireless champion of the law. In 1748,

indeed, he took personal charge of a Special Commission against Sussex smugglers, arguing that, 'nothing but an active zeal, manifested by public acts, can give a check to these dangerous outrages and barbarous and inhuman murderers'. In the mock holdup, Richmond had shown himself to be like that cheeky rapscallion, his father, and loved every minute of it. Later he was horrified, and seized the opportunity to show himself the reformed son. By all accounts he pursued the lawbreakers with a vengeance, determined to cleanse the county and himself at the same time.

The Duke's other great love, passed on to his children, and closely related to the rituals both of Masonry and the Court, was the theatre. The Court was, of course, the most theatrical of all

W illiam Hogarth's *A Performance of the Indian Emperor or the Conquest of Mexico* (1732). The play was an old favourite by Dryden, the youthful players from the best families. Nine-year-old Caroline Lennox, who played a major role, is second from the right on the stage. The 2nd Duke of Richmond is in the foreground leaning over his wife's chair, the image of the affectionate husband and attentive father. A bust of Isaac Newton, revered by the Duke and his circle, surveys the scene.

public sites, with its levees, birthdays and presentations, and it made very good drama, re-enactments of successive coronations playing on the London stage for decades. Richmond and his fellow courtiers lived such an inherently theatrical life that for many of them the stage proved irresistible. The Lennoxes were all, from an early age, frequent visitors to Covent Garden and Drury Lane, where they had permanent boxes.

The theatre also mirrored aristocratic life in its intermingling of the public and the private. Covent Garden and Drury Lane were places where the public and the private existed simultaneously and side by side. Sitting in their enclosed box, the Duke and his family were cut off from and yet surrounded by the rest of the audience, which included not only aristocrats, but anybody who could afford to pay the admission price. Like them they were both spectacle and audience. As individuals they watched the actors on the stage and the people around them in the boxes and the pit. As a collective they were themselves a show, gazed at as representatives of the aristocracy by others. So, in the theatre, aristocrats both subsumed and crystallized their identity, never for a moment becoming private individuals, and yet participating in the drama, watching the play like anybody else.

If the theatre offered a universe of ritual and convention in which an audience watched the play while sitting in the public gaze, it was also a place where one set of rituals could be set aside for another, and the courtiers could become actors. Watching the stage was not enough. Richmond, along with many of his associates, wanted to be on it and to swap the courtier for the thespian. So he built private theatres for himself at Richmond House and at Goodwood, where he, his family and friends assumed innumerable roles in tragedies and farces acted largely for their own entertainment.

No one was too young to be enrolled in the play; at the age of eight, Caroline Lennox was already strutting the boards. It was given to her, in an epilogue to a play performed in 1732, to connect aristocratic life with dramatic performance and both to the pervading English sense that 'all the world's a stage':

You, dear Mama, whose fondness has this night
Heard with so much patience and with some delight,
To us, with pride, will your applause be shown,
Our virtues are infant copies of your own.
The time shall come when we, mature of age,
Shall act your parts upon a nobler stage.

Little Caroline was also painted as an actress in a performance of *The Indian Emperor*. Hogarth's picture shows a group of children acting in Dryden's play before a private audience in the

Royal mint, including various members of the Royal family and the Duke and Duchess of Richmond. A bust of the presiding genius, Isaac Newton, looks down on the show, and the Duke of Richmond is shown just as Horace Walpole once described him, leaning affectionately over his wife's chair. Caroline Lennox is a tiny figure in pink gesturing out from the action towards her parents, playing her part as she would be expected to live her life, on view and on stage.

The 2nd Duke of Richmond rounded off his character as a Whig gentleman and a public figure (albeit one who stood aside from party politics, which he thought of as vulgar) by developing his interest in new kinds of scientific knowledge. He was described as having a passion for 'all sorts of natural knowledge' and he saw himself above all as a collector – of animals,

OPPOSITE

The very elaborate shell cottage in the grounds of Goodwood House, designed by the 2nd Duchess of Richmond with the help of her daughters Caroline and Emily in the 1730s. The Duchess and her girls would have laid out the designs – presumably over sketches on sheets of paper – and then turned over the work of transferring them to the walls to workers from the Goodwood estate.

plants, curiosities, shells, statues and ideas, especially those of Newton and his followers in the natural sciences. In part the Duke's interests were entirely in keeping with contemporary and fashionable notions about the importance of studying the natural order of the universe and the animal kingdom: it was desirable for gentlemen to be seen to be patrons of scientific investigation and the dissemination of new knowledge. But as much as a necessary part of a courtier's repertoire of habits, the Duke's fondness for collecting and patronage of science were the response of a careful man to his own disorderly past; the better arranged the universe and the world around him, the more secure he could feel that his father's unruly spirit was laid to rest.

Thus when Richmond sat to the painter Philips in the late 1740s, he presented himself to the viewer as both courtier and collector. He wore the royal blue ribbon of the Order of the Garter and stood in front of bookshelves in the library of Richmond House in Whitehall, with the panoply of modern knowledge ranged behind him, and in the entrance a draped classical figure which gestured to his membership of the Society of Antiquaries and his love of collecting.

Richmond's favourite area of acquisition, however, was the natural world, especially the plant and animal kingdoms. Isaac Newton, who,

the Duke said 'every man of learning' must hold in 'the utmost veneration', had, so the story ran, brought understanding to the study of the physical universe. Now scientists were following his lead with the classification and ordering of flora and fauna. Richmond was an active member of the Royal Society; he patronized research into marine life in the Solent off the Sussex coast, and from the 1730s onwards he amassed a costly collection of plants and animals at Goodwood itself. Richmond's menagerie was not the first of its kind in Britain, but it was one of the biggest and best housed, occupying specially heated quarters in his park. In the warmed underground cages lived at various times five wolves, two tigers, two lions, three bears, two leopards, a chimpanzee, three racoons, an armadillo and a host of lesser birds and beasts. The 'flesh eaters', as a note in the Goodwood archive puts it, consumed 70lb of meat a day, while the vegetarians got through three large loaves of bread along with their greenstuff.

Along with these animals, obliging sea captains brought seeds and shells to Goodwood. The seeds that germinated were planted out in the park – acacias, maples, tulip trees and ilex among them – while the shells were consigned to the Duchess and her daughters. The girls and their mother sorted and classified the shells before assembling them into intricate designs to cover the walls of a shell grotto in the park and

The Thames from Richmond House, painted by Canaletto in 1747. Richmond House, standing roughly between the present site of the cenotaph and the Embankment, was built by the 2nd Duke in the 1730s. Looking east across the river and north west up Whitehall, it commanded one of London's best prospects, and boasted the fine terrace overlooking the river that Canaletto paints here dotted with members of the Lennox family strolling in the morning sun.

to celebrate nature's diversity, man's sea-faring prowess and women's artifice.

The menagerie, the spreading trees in the park and the rococo designs of the shell cottage were all evidence of the commercial and military spread of British might. As the empire grew, so did the Duke's collections, as if the world over which Britain held sway was reassembled in his park to be studied, marvelled at and controlled.

Along with his collections and his careful Court career, Richmond was determined to have country and town houses that reflected his social position and his own love of stability and order. He remodelled the old-fashioned Jacobean exterior of Goodwood, and added a stuccoed and pedimented front that faced south towards the town of Chichester and housed several imposing suites of rooms decorated in the fashionable classical style. Perhaps designed by Matthew Brettingham, it was modelled on William Kent's Devonshire House and intended to present the Duke as a man of taste and discernment. His ambitions in London were grander, for it was here that his role as a public man was most often played and most visible. Demolishing the small house in Whitehall he had inherited, which, in its ramshackle dilapidation, was all too reminiscent of his father's and grandfather's merry moral decay, he built in the 1730s an imposing three-storeyed pedimented residence that combined grandeur

and comfort in the modern classical style. Designed by Lord Burlington, it was built between 1730 and 1734. A decade later the Duke commissioned the Italian artist Canaletto to paint two views from its windows – one looking over the Thames, the other up Whitehall – that would emphasize the family's position at the heart of London's social, commercial and political world.

By the 1740s when Canaletto arrived in England, he had been known to the Duke for two decades. In 1722, even before he succeeded to the dukedom, Richmond began to execute a project that he had probably conceived while on the Grand Tour, a series of allegorical tomb paintings, 'Monuments to the Remembrance of a Set of British Worthies', that was intended to commemorate leading figures of the Protestant cause and the Hanoverian Succession. His continental agent was Owen McSwiney, a failed theatrical impresario who made a living acting as middle man between British patrons and Italian painters. Ten tomb paintings eventually arrived at Goodwood and hung in the dining-room there. Canaletto had a hand in several of them and the Duke also bought a number of his Venetian cityscapes. So it was not surprising that when Canaletto came to London in 1746, McSwiney, by then in Britain himself, passed him on to Richmond. Canaletto's two magnificent views more than repaid the Duke's patronage.

As he does in his Venetian paintings, Canaletto plays with perspective and mass to satisfy both the grandeur demanded by his subject and the desires of his patrons. *The Thames and the City of London from Richmond House*, completed in 1747, alters perspective and the ordering of buildings in such a way as to emphasize London's role as a great commercial city like Venice. By notably sharpening the bend in the Thames between Westminster and the Port of London, Canaletto not only makes it seem more like the curvaceous Grand Canal, and London more like Venice, but also brings the City and St Paul's Cathedral right into the middle of the picture rather than leaving them to the left of centre where nature put them.

Commerce, whence came the Richmond fortune, and the Protestant religion, represented by the dramatically enlarged cathedral which rides over the City like a secular marble palace, are moved to the picture's heart. Yet Canaletto never forgot to add domestic touches. As the rowers on the royal barges strain upstream on the river, members of the Richmond family stroll on the terrace, and white-painted wooden benches placed against the west-facing boundary wall invite the viewer to sit down and enjoy the sun moving round beyond the pleasure gardens of Vauxhall and the villages of Richmond and Kew.

The same dual sense of grandeur and intimacy is apparent in the painting's companion, *Whitehall and the Privy Garden*. In the background, exaggerated again for formal and family effect, rises the bulk of Inigo Jones's Banqueting House begun by the Duke's great-grandfather Charles I, while in the foreground we look down on the Duke himself, being greeted by a servant as he comes into the stableyard. Around him in the stableyard chickens scratch about and a washing line hangs waiting for work. At the back of the stable block is the open door from which his eldest daughter Caroline slipped out of the house into the Privy Garden when she had eloped with Henry Fox three years before.

The Duke and Duchess of Richmond intended for their children arranged marriages and Court lives very much like their own. But like many parents they found that their children – and especially their favourite children – had ideas that didn't fit in with this cosy plan. They discovered this in the most dramatic way when Caroline defied their wishes and married a man they thought in every way unsuitable.

The tiny actress of Hogarth's *The Indian Emperor* had, by 1743, grown into an intense, anxious young woman, independent in spirit and highly intelligent. Like most of her contemporaries, Caroline was a fervent believer in the utility and value of reason, and she was also by temperament a lover of legalistic arguments and moralizing epithets. But she was at the same time highly emotional and committed to the life of the imagination and the exercise of passion. The hallmark of her personality was, perhaps, a passionate pessimism that clouded even the happiest moments of her life; yet, characteristically, her way of allaying anxiety was to demand more, not less, understanding of the 'human species', as she called it and to try to use reason to understand life's vagaries. 'My dearest sister', she wrote to Emily in 1768, 'how we hurry away with one thing or another the minute allotted us here. Surely were there not something better to come it would be a foolish affair.' Anxiety always coloured her dreams of contentment or joy. 'Human events are so subject to disappointment,

OPPOSITE
Canaletto's view looking across the Privy Garden, the old garden of the Whitehall Palace, which had, by the eighteenth century, become an open public space. By the time Canaletto painted the Duke coming into his stableyard, Caroline had already fled out of it to elope with Henry Fox.

she noted in 1760, 'is generally to have too good an opinion of the world, and the worst part of growing old is being undeceived in that point.'

It was perhaps no surprise to her parents that Caroline was still unmarried at 20, an age by which many aristocratic girls already had several children. But when she eloped with Henry Fox in 1744, after months of secret courtship, they were far more angered by her choice than relieved that she was no longer on the shelf. Henry Fox, after all, was a man without title, large fortune, property or pedigree. He was everything, indeed, that Caroline's parents didn't want.

There were connections between the Foxes and Lennoxes, though, connections of which the Duke and Duchess did not much wish to be reminded. Henry's father, Sir Stephen Fox, had been an old friend of Louise de Kéroualle, and like her he came into his fame and fortune as a servant of Charles II. Stephen Fox had been born in Wiltshire in 1627, educated at Salisbury Grammar School and brought into the household of Charles, Prince of Wales in 1640. After the Royalist defeat by Cromwell, he followed Charles to France. There he managed the finances of the royal household in exile. By judiciously husbanding and investing the money entrusted to him, and by forging valuable connections with foreign bankers, he not only kept the crown-in-exile afloat but also laid the foundations of a fortune for himself. When the

I really fear to please myself with thoughts of any future happiness.' She loved to ape a group she professed to despise, men and women who 'pretended to wit', and she was adept at turning out the sort of nostrums about the human condition that were produced by the French *philosophes* who formed her opinion and provided her favourite reading matter. 'The fault of youth',

Henry Fox painted by Antonio David in Rome in the 1730s, when he was the lover of Mrs Strangways Horner, a position Lord Shaftesbury described as being 'more to the credit of his vigour than his morals'. Fox had two mentors in his youth: Mrs Strangways Horner's daughter and the bisexual Whig politician Lord Hervey. He repaid the interest of both by arranging the marriage of Mrs Strangways Horner's daughter to Lord Hervey's lover – who just happened to be his own brother.

Opposite Lady Caroline Lennox in masquerade costume, a pastel by William Hoare, probably drawn in the 1740s. A young woman of unconventional tastes, she loved everything old-fashioned – old houses, ancient history, old people and a husband almost twenty years older than herself.

L ord Hervey and his friends, by William Hogarth, 1738. This conversation piece shows Lord Hervey gesturing towards his friend Henry Fox. Fox had recently been made Surveyor-General of the King's Works and holds up the plan of a Royal building. His brother Stephen Fox is sitting at the table surrounded by other men in their circle – the Duke of Marlborough, Lord Wilmington and perhaps the very cleric who officiated at the wedding of Stephen and Elizabeth Strangways Horner.

monarchy was restored in 1660, Fox's loyalty and administrative brilliance were rewarded with the lucrative office of Paymaster General of the Forces, and he was knighted by Charles II into the bargain.

Stephen Fox was not only comfortable and honoured in retirement, he was also extremely spry. At the age of 76 he married one of his daughter's friends Christian Hope, a woman who, as he put it, 'was very helpful to me by reading and thereby entertaining my spare hours in my retirement, with such advantage that I thought her conversation would be useful to my old age.' Fox professed to being as surprised as his friends at the birth of his son Stephen a year later, but three more children confirmed the old man's vigour: Henry and Christian, born in 1705, and Charlotte, born in 1708, when Sir Stephen was 81 years old.

Stephen and Henry Fox clung to their father's Toryism and Stuart sympathies after the Hanoverian Succession and their father's death in 1716, and their prospects did not look good. Their mother, ailing herself, was worried about them: they were both adrift, bred to be politicians and crown servants, but without any patrons or hopes of preferment in the new Whig regime. On her death-bed Lady Fox called all her children into her room and read them a stern moral lecture about the future, assuming, Henry wrote, 'a more than ordinary majestic air'. Her

advice haunted Henry, as she intended it should. 'When I am gone', she said, 'it will shew your love and hate to me as you obey or disobey my instructions.' Lady Fox ordered Henry to fight off the manifold temptations that were bound to come his way: 'take care to avoid ill company. If you don't you are gone, for by it many young men are ruined … You'll learn to swear, to drink, to rake about, to game and at last to be ruined by those you unhappily think your friends.'

Soon after his mother's death, Henry Fox went up to Christ Church, Oxford, and set about proving the truth of her observation. He became gregarious and garrulous; he loved company and particularly the company of brilliant and witty men. Soon he gained a reputation for brilliance himself; he had a prodigious memory and astounded his friends by his recitations of Latin verse. Once, to win a bet, he reeled off 50 lines of Ovid without a mistake and without preparation. He gambled, had affairs, wrote reams of bad verse, ate and drank and whored. He lost his faith and gained a reputation for cynicism.

When he came down from Oxford, Fox settled at Redlynch, his brother's Wiltshire country seat for want of anything better to do. He played the life of a country gentleman to the hilt, shooting and gambling and striding about over the fields. Even so, he was restless. His intelligence and his tremendous ambition

for worldly success were thwarted and without direction. In the nick of time he met Lord Hervey, a perfect and willing recipient of his wit and charm. Hervey had just been elected to Parliament. He was a staunch Whig and had good connections at Court. When the reign of George II began in 1727, Hervey's standing with the crown meant that he was well placed to act as patron to any young man who caught his eye. Hervey met Fox at Bath, which, by the 1720s, was already a place notable for its social informality and amorous intriguing. Bath was only 21 miles from Redlynch, and Henry used

to go there to find women, games of cards, drink and conversation. Fox dazzled Hervey with his brilliance and tantalized him with his reserve. Both men enjoyed the game of cat and mouse that followed. Fox retreated to Redlynch. Hervey pursued him with letters, grumbling that Fox gave him as little sustenance as the fashionable Bath doctor, Cheyne, who advised starvation as the route to health. 'I insist on being told what you do from morning to night in the country, and I would now and then be glad to be told what you think. I have unbounded curiosity with regard to those I love, but your reservedness I

Stephen Fox – later Stephen Fox-Strangways – with his son in the fields of his Dorset estate, painted by a local artist, Brown, in 1744. When he became Earl of Ilchester in 1756, Emily wrote mischievously to Henry Fox, 'I am glad your brother is made an earl. He is a sweet man, worth a thousand of you, much better humoured, ten thousand times better bred, much livelier, and I believe full as clever.'

fear will make it live upon as slender diet as a patient of Dr. Cheyne's.' Hervey's amorous attentions were soon diverted on to Henry's brother Stephen, with whom he had an affair that lasted many years. He and Henry settled into a jocular friendship that revolved around wit and women and purely epistolary flirtation. Fox had a talent for writing flirtatious letters and he learned a good deal from Hervey, who was a master of the art.

While he flattered Fox's virility and learning, Hervey was also changing his young friend's political allegiances. Fox loved to talk politics – 'I hear nothing but petitions, journals, treaties, alliances', Hervey complained to Stephen in 1728 – but he wanted political power too. He realized that he could never hope for office as a Tory, so he switched parties, became a Whig and was elected to Hervey's seat of Hinden in 1735. After 10 years of waiting in the wings, he was able to start his political career.

It was not only Lord Hervey who was helping Fox up the ladder. He had another powerful figure working on his behalf, Susannah Strangways Horner, a landowner's wife with whom he had started an affair in 1728. It was hinted that Mrs Strangways Horner gave Fox money in return for sex and entertainment. Lord Chesterfield claimed that she was 'a very salacious English woman whose liberality retrieved his fortune with several circumstances

more to the credit of his vigour than his morals'. Fox certainly spent a good deal of time with Mrs Strangways Horner, mainly on the Continent where she travelled about, estranged from her husband, a rich Tory squire who refused to leave the West Country. Nominally Fox was her 'trustee', managing her finances. In fact he was her lover and companion. He also acted as mentor and occasional tutor to Mrs Strangways Horner's daughter, Elizabeth. Early in the 1730s they went to Spain and Italy and travelled about the south of France. In the summer of 1733 Fox was back at Redlynch. Lord Hervey observed him there, gloomy and bad tempered. The whole party decamped to Goodwood in July, when Henry and Lady Hervey gamely performed in the Duke of Richmond's mock highway robbery.

Fox was obviously restless in the 1730s, see-sawing between Somerset, London and the Continent. He was back in Paris in the autumn of 1733, with an introduction to Voltaire in his pocket, but returned to England again in December in time to spend Christmas at Goodwood. Then he went back to France again. To his friends he seemed distant and distracted. 'Whilst you are talking to him he will be reading, and whilst he is reading he will be thinking of something else; by which means you will know nothing of him nor he of his book', wrote Hervey to Stephen. In fact Fox did not

utterly fritter his time away on the Continent. He perfected his French and Italian, he read a good deal, he visited his father's old friend Louise de Kéroualle in her Aubigny château, and in Rome he had himself painted by Antonio David. In the full-length portrait, Fox stares fixedly out at the viewer, his right hand extended on the barrel of an enormous and priapic gun. A servant, obsequious but disregarded, stoops to tie his master's shoelaces, while in the foreground of the painting two huge hounds, their collars emblazoned with Fox's name, strain at the leash, noses up and snarling, almost bursting out of the canvas. The painting was Fox's attempt to portray himself as a gentleman in command of the world. But it succeeded better in showing him still nervous about his social position and replete with barely tamed aggression and energy. Back home, he served his administrative apprenticeship in the calm green pastures of Mrs Strangways Horner's estate in Dorset, and he also took the trouble to pass on his mother's death-bed advice to his young pupil.

Acting as Elizabeth's tutor was an office charged with irony of the kind that Fox enjoyed. Exhorting the little girl to virtue while he luxuriated in vice with her mother was calculated to feed both Fox's cynicism and his sentimentality. He loved children and, sporadically, he enjoyed teaching Elizabeth. But he also wallowed in the fact that he was a bad man teaching her to be good. One of the assignments he gave Elizabeth was to write about the folly of wicked behaviour. 'Look around you', he urged, 'and you will see the covetous, unhappy from those very riches which they wretchedly and uncharitably hoard or by wicked means obtain. You will see the undiscreet [sic] losing their pleasures thro' those very indiscretions by which they aim at pleasure; just as the intemperate lose their appetites by the excesses they commit to please them.' And to whom should Elizabeth show this homily from her excessive and covetous tutor? Her indiscreet mother, of course. It was this sort of game with which Fox amused himself in the barren years of the 1730s. It was harmless enough and held just enough titillation to keep him from bored and weary melancholy.

This was Fox's game in 1735. A year later he had made huge strides in cynicism. With breathtaking disregard for moral probity, he helped Mrs Horner arrange a secret marriage between Elizabeth, who had just turned 13, and his 32-year-old brother Stephen who was still in love with Lord Hervey and sharing a house with him in London. Hervey himself helped arrange the match; he thought that like his own surprisingly happy marriage, it would make no difference to his affair with Stephen. Mrs Strangways Horner was determined to join two large fortunes and two neighbouring estates.

Stephen raised no objection and Henry was happy to help Hervey and Stephen and his lover all at once. Indeed everybody was delighted, except perhaps Mr Strangways Horner, and he was deliberately kept in the dark, and little Elizabeth, whose feelings were the last thing on anybody's mind. But the reverberations of the marriage were unexpected. One hundred and fifty years later it was still such a byword for scandal and cynicism in the West Country that Thomas Hardy, who collected stories of people being sold off for one reason or another, wrote a novel about it. More surprising still, it ended Stephen's long-standing affair with Hervey and made Elizabeth and Stephen very happy. After three years of living apart, they settled down at Redlynch to a quiet country life. Stephen gradually abandoned London and Parliament; he even stopped bothering to come up for the season, preferring domestic felicity, guns, dogs, children and his cosy study.

Even as Stephen was retreating into the shade, Henry was biding his time, waiting for his turn in the limelight. In 1737, again through the offices of Lord Hervey, he got his chance. Hervey got him the post of Surveyor General of the King's Works, a job worth £1,100 a year. Henry became responsible for the upkeep of all the royal palaces, parks, gardens and roads. Although Hervey jokingly called him 'Neglector of the King's Works', Fox performed his duties

with competence and zeal. During the 1740s he moved up fast in the Whig hierarchy. By 1742 he had impressed the government ministers sufficiently to be advanced to a position in the Treasury. There he demonstrated his administrative abilities and his financial acumen. He also began to perfect an evident skill in the tricky business of parliamentary management, wheeling and dealing behind the scenes in clubs and drawing-rooms to secure government majorities for important pieces of legislation. Then Fox came into his own, exerting all his charm, trading on his wit and *bonhomie*, delighted to find himself the centre of attention and still capable of being a tough negotiator if necessary. By the early 1740s his inveterate gregariousness was coming to the service of his political ambition and acumen. Fox began to sense his strength and flex his political muscles. But he was also emotionally on the loose, estranged from both Hervey and Mrs Strangways Horner, and increasingly envious of his brother's domestic happiness.

It was then that Henry Fox began to think of Caroline not just as the nervously intelligent girl he had known from her childhood, but as his future companion. In a few months he had succeeded not only in capturing her heart but also in making her his wife. Caroline had not studied the 'human species' without effect and she had chosen wisely. Their marriage was

RIGHT

Lady Emily Lennox, in masquerade costume, drawn by William Hoare in the late 1740s. She was beautiful and much adored from childhood to old age. 'Life to me is nothing without you', her first husband wrote, while her second told her when she was eighty-one that she was, 'the first and reigning object of my thought and feeling'.

famously happy, and Fox went on to realize nearly all of his political ambitions – although the office of Prime Minister eluded him – to become an earl and to amass a fortune, rumoured to be nearly £400,000 as Paymaster General of the Armed Forces in the Seven Years War of 1756 to 1763.

As Paymaster, Fox held large amounts of money which he was entitled to lend back to the government for his own profit. This was a risky venture – government stocks might collapse leaving the Paymaster massively indebted. But Fox used his political acumen to anticipate market movements and, as he explained in a statement written in the face of public hostility to his activities, made a fortune. 'The sudden rise of stocks has made me richer than I ever intended or desir'd to be', he wrote in 1762. 'Obloquy generally attends money so got, but with how much reason in all cases this simple account of my gains shows. The Government borrows money at 20% discount; I am not consulted or concern'd in making the bargain. I have as Pay Master great sums in my hands which, not applicable to any present use, must either lye dead in the Bank, or be employed by me. I lend this to the government in 1761. A peace is thought certain. I am not in the least consulted, but my very bad opinion of Mr Pitt makes me think it will not be concluded: I sell out and gain greatly. In 1762, I lend again; a

peace comes, in which again I am not consulted, & I again gain greatly.'

Although the residue of Fox's fortune was completely dissipated by his sons Stephen – always called Ste – and Charles James's gambling, much was spent before he died. He and Caroline moved into the large (and very old-fashioned) Jacobean mansion of Holland House, on the western edge of London, soon after their marriage. They went on to acquire a gaudily splendid town house in Piccadilly for the huge sum of £16,000 in 1762, and they bought land and property in the West Country and the country estate of Kingsgate near Broadstairs in Kent, where Henry Fox amused himself in retirement building follies, 'ruins' and a modernized re-creation of a Roman country villa. Thus Caroline, marrying against her parents' wishes, lived in just as much contentment and far greater luxury than they had ever done.

The second of the Richmond children's marriages – that of their favourite Emily to the Earl of Kildare in 1747 – was scarcely more to their liking than Caroline's runaway match with Fox. James Fitzgerald's problem was not, like Fox's, lack of title, money or status. Moreover, unlike Fox, he was young and handsome. His difficulty was first that he was Irish and second that he was proud of it. The Richmonds' dislike of an Irish connection for their daughter was a common enough objection at the time, and English brides generally had to be paid for with a good many Irish pounds, but Fitzgerald was no run-of-the-mill absentee Whig landlord. He was, as he put it in a memorial written for the monarch in 1753, 'the eldest peer of the realm, by descent, as lineally sprung from the ancient and august blood of the noble Earl of Kildare, who came over under the invincible banner of your august predecessor Henry II, when his arms conquered the Kingdom of Ireland' and went on 'that though they were first sent over with letters patent under Henry II's banner to conquer this Kingdom, yet by the inheritance of lands, by intermarriages with the princesses of the Kingdom, they became powerful, and might have conquered for themselves, notwithstanding which, their allegiance was such that, on our sovereign's mandates to stop the progress of war, we obeyed, and relinquished our title of conquest, laid down our arms, and received that monarch with due homage and allegiance.'

From these ponderous ramblings, salient features of Kildare's character and responsibilities stand out. His family, the Fitzgeralds, or Geraldines as they were popularly known, had indeed first come to Ireland under the banner of Henry II. But they operated more as independent conquerors who owed a barely nominal allegiance to the English crown than as soldiers employed on the King's business. Large tracts of fertile land

in the centre of the country fell into their hands and the Geraldines rapidly established themselves as a permanent presence. They collected and accepted tributes from local kings, married local women and hired poets to weave fantastic stories of their prowess. Until their power was broken by force in 1540, the Geraldines ruled as colonial princes and warlords, becoming, as time went on, less and less like the waves of settlers who came after them and more and more like the kings with whom they treated. After the Reformation and Henry VIII's troops had deposed them, the Geraldines had to claw their way slowly back to prominence and wealth. They became Protestants and supporters of the English crown and settled down as landlords who always claimed to be more sympathetic to their tenants than their absentee neighbours of more recent settlement. Wealth came back with the boom in Irish agriculture in the eighteenth century, the rise in trade with the Atlantic colonies and the growth of Dublin as the second city of the British empire.

When he proposed to Emily, Kildare had a rent roll of getting on for £15,000 a year, a London town house and two immensely grand houses in Ireland: Leinster House, still under construction on the south side of Dublin, and Carton, a massive Palladian mansion a few miles west of the city on his Kildare estate. He had no need to be frugal, and knowing that the Duke of Richmond would drive a hard bargain for his

daughter on the grounds of his Irishness and his lack of political or familial connections in England, he set out as he meant to go on. Not only would the terms of the marriage settlement be extremely favourable to Emily, but the Earl hastened to assure the Duke that she would get everything she wanted, just as she had done in her childhood. Slipping – to his own disadvantage – into a hint of brogue, the Earl wrote to assuage the Duke's hostility during the negotiations, saying, 'Sure I can propose no happiness for myself if she does not share it equally with me, and I flatter myself that no part of my character, or actions of my life can contradict this assertion. I must add this truth, which I beg your Grace will believe, that, without regard to settlements, my own honour and the strong tie of affection and esteem will not suffer me to let Lady Emily want any affluence that is fit for her, and my own wife, nor even what in any kind can make her happy.'

Kildare was made to wait a humiliating 18 months with good grace. But eventually he got his bride, her parents being unable to think of any more objections, beyond her extreme youth, that would not provoke a duel. Kildare kept his word too: Emily never did want for anything. She matured into, and remained, a famously 'expensive' woman, whose major pastime during her marriage to Kildare (or the Duke of Leinster as he became in 1766) and between producing 19 children, was spending money.

The Duke and Duchess of Richmond gradually became reconciled to Emily's marriage, helped along by a flurry of charming letters she sent from Ireland describing her pregnancy and the birth of her first child and heir, George, Lord Offaly, in 1749. The Duke slowly came round to Caroline's marriage, too: he had been a confidant of Henry Fox's for some time, and was secretly glad to be able to pick up the reins of their friendship. Besides, by 1749 he had three grandsons who would not only head his daughter's new families, but also, if necessary, secure the Richmond dynasty as well. The future looked serene, and in 1749 the Duke celebrated his won happiness, his family's new unity and peace in Europe with a party and firework display, in the presence of the King and much of the Court. A print was made of the occasion showing the Royal barge on the river, the nobility on Richmond House terrace and the fireworks rushing skywards between them. Little more than a year later the Duke died. The Duchess did not long survive him, dying herself in 1751.

When the Duke died, his 15-year-old son Charles became 3rd Duke of Richmond and titular head of the Lennox family, assuming responsibility for them in the wider world and for the reputation of the family as a whole. He had few family members to take any sort of charge of for many years, however, because by the

LEFT

A view of the Fireworks and Illuminations at his His Grace the Duke of Richmond's at Whitehall, anon., 1749. Richmond House appears on the extreme left of the painting. The fireworks were launched both from the terrace and from boats on the river, where the King and other members of the Royal Family watched from the Royal barge.

terms of his parents' will, his younger sisters Louisa aged nearly eight, Sarah, aged six and Cecilia just one were sent to live in Ireland with Emily, only to be returned to England when they needed to be presented at Court and launched on the London marriage market.

The 3rd Duke, who married Lady Mary Bruce in 1757, aspired to be a more active and influential politician than his father. He matured from a gauche but promiscuous Westminster schoolboy into a clever man, albeit one who – so his sisters complained – preferred to ride rather than read and who remained ill-read if well-informed about the issues of the day. But he

Lady Mary Bruce, 3rd Duchess of Richmond, painted in Turkish masquerade costume by Angelica Kauffmann about 1775, and the 3rd Duke, at the age of twenty in 1755, painted in Rome on the Grand Tour by Pompeo Batoni. Their marriage was reasonably successful, although the Duchess never had any children. Caroline started by finding her droll and pleasant, but by the mid-1760s declared that she was irremediably philistine and insufficiently cosmopolitan and went on to blame her for leading Sarah astray at the end of the decade.

The Tapestry Room at Goodwood House. Built by the 3rd Duke to designs by James Wyatt, it was created to display the Gobelins tapestries and some of the furniture the Duke brought back from Paris after his embassy there in 1765–6. The Duke was not a particularly successful ambassador, while the Duchess, Caroline noticed censoriously, could not speak proper French, declined to invite French people to her home and surrounded herself with Englishmen.

OPPOSITE

A reproduction of the awning erected in Green Park for members of the Royal Family for the King's fireworks in 1759. The display, accompanied by Handel's *Music fot the Royal Fireworks*, was a disaster, and part of the specially constructed pavilion burned to the ground. When the scene was filmed for *Aristocrats*, the Irish weather added a rainstorm that obligingly supplemented the mood of disappointment.

was pompous and over-deliberate, unable 0to convert his thoughtfulness into political acumen. 'I pass in the world for very obstinate, wrong-headed and tenacious of my own opinions', he wrote with accurate self-assessment to Edmund Burke in 1772. Others agreed, and his political career was less successful than his intelligence merited.

The Duke inhabited the radical wing of the Whig party until the the early 1780s, supporting the rebel American colonists against the British crown, declaring in 1775 that their behaviour was 'neither treason nor rebellion, but is perfectly justifiable in every possible political and moral sense', and sailing his yacht through the British fleet in the Solent with the rebel flag flying at its masthead. In 1780 he introduced a reform Bill into Parliament that proposed equal electoral districts (thus doing away with the complex and corrupt borough system), annual parliamentary elections and universal male suffrage. In the struggle between William Pitt the Younger and his own nephew Charles James Fox, however, Richmond took Pitt's side, perhaps unable to countenance being under the aegis of his sister's son and a man a generation younger than himself. When Fox went into opposition in 1784, Richmond stayed in government with Pitt for almost two decades, serving for much of that time as Master of the Ordnance.

Richmond's relations with his immediate

family were not much better than those with politicians. Through the years he see-sawed up and down in his siblings' estimation. He was sometimes generous, sometimes tetchy, withholding or withdrawing his approval of their actions in ways that seemed arbitrary and overbearing. His relationship with Caroline and Emily was distant, with Louisa relatively serene and with Sarah extremely stormy. He disapproved of her first marriage to Charles Bunbury and refused to pay for her wedding dress, a gesture of approbation expected of heads of families. Yet he tacitly condoned her subsequent affair with Lord William Gordon – indeed it seems to have been incubated under the lamps of the card-tables of Richmond House – and offered her a home at Goodwood after she had left both her husband and her lover.

It was during the period of her social ostracism, indeed, that Sarah's relations with her brother were at their best. In 1776, when she had been living at Goodwood for nearly seven years, the Duke visited Emily at the family château of Aubigny in France, where she herself had retreated after her elopement with and marriage to William Ogilvie. 'You cannot think', wrote Sarah to Emily, 'how often I read your letters in general, but particularly that from Aubigny where you let yourself run on about my brother. In this world there is nothing so pleasant as having those one loves love each

other; and the happiness it has given me that you should love my brother as I do, is not to be told. I don't think you ever knew him rightly before, and the idea that you would find him such a treasure as he is, was one of the things that pleased me so much in this visit to you. I am sure that nobody is more to be depended on; and where he can show friendship and kindness,

I am always *sure* of him.' Five years later she had decisively changed her mind. The Duke was furious when she left the obscurity of Goodwood for marriage to an impoverished career soldier, George Napier, and relations between them never recovered again.

The 3rd Duke inherited his father's fondness for Goodwood and spent more and more time there as his interest in political reform and day-to-day London intrigue declined. He liked Goodwood much better than his sisters. Caroline complained that 'the air is cold and sharp there', and hardly ever went down, while Sarah wrote in 1779, when her stock was beginning to decline because of her flirtation with Napier, 'Goodwood is a very dull place for young people; the master and mistress are always busy, and hunting is the only amusement'.

RIGHT
The château at Aubigny in France inherited by the 1st Duke from his mother Louise de Kéroualle. Sequestered during the French Revolution, it was restored to the family in 1815, but finally sold in the 1840s.
OPPOSITE The 2nd Duke and Duchess – Julian Fellowes and Diane Fletcher – with their family in the 1740s. The future 3rd Duke – William Sparks – sits next to his father. Caroline – Serena Gordon – stands behind him and Emily – Hayley Griffiths – is next to her.

Mostly the 3rd Duke was busy about renovation and building and about enlarging his estate. He began in a relatively modest way, building a new drawing-room to designs by James Wyatt in the early 1770s. It was created to house the collection of Gobelins tapestries and French furniture he acquired when he was ambassador to the Court of Louis XV in 1765–6, and boasts an extraordinary marble fireplace constructed of two standing classical figures in place of the usual arrangement of columns and mantel, by John Bacon, a sculptor known more for his tombs than for decorative pieces.

For three decades the 3rd Duke only tinkered, but at the beginning of the next century he embarked on a massive programme of building precipitated by the spectacular burning down of Richmond House in Whitehall – uninsured and therefore irreplaceable – in 1791. The works of art had been salvaged from the blaze and the Duke needed somewhere to put them. Wyatt designed two new wings at obtuse angles with towers at both ends of each wing to unify the whole composition. The towers, looking like four giant domed salt-shakers, certainly brought the disparate parts of the building together, and gave the house a unique, if slightly priapic, appearance. The building was still unfinished when the Duke died in 1806, leaving his nephew and heir the makings of a magnificent house as well as huge debts.

Town Life

'THE LIFE OF A FINE LONDON LADY produces but very flimsy materials for society out of it', Sarah Lennox wrote in middle age to her old friend Susan Fox-Strangways. Her sisters were fond of airing other complaints about Britain's capital city, especially its hurry and expense. But with the exception of Louisa, who was a confirmed country dweller, they all secretly warmed to the attractions of town life: the balls and assemblies, the theatre and the pleasure gardens, the shopping and the dressing up, the late hours, the intrigue, the gambling and the fun. 'My dear Netty', wrote Sarah using her favourite nickname for Susan in 1766 when she was a young married woman pleased to be back in town after a prolonged stay in her country house of Barton in Suffolk, 'I have been in town about a month and am not settled yet, for I have not had a moment's time to myself. The hurry of this town is inconceivable, for I declare I have been only once to the play, opera and oratorio, to very few assemblies, and yet I cannot find a moment's time to myself.'

Social life was not all parties and card tables. Much of it was centred on more informal family gatherings, especially as time went on and the Lennox family grew. London became the easiest place to meet for such a dispersed and large group, and after half a life-time away, Sarah came back there in her old age, realizing that it was only there that she could easily see her children, siblings, in-laws and other relatives. Forty years after complaining to Susan of the bustle of the capital, she wrote of it again to Susan in exactly the same tone of exasperation and pleasure. 'I live in a perfect hurry', she wrote in 1805, when she was 60

ABOVE

Holland House, Kensington, in the mid-nineteenth century, by John Wykeman Archer, unaltered since Caroline and Henry Fox moved in a century earlier. By the mid-nineteenth century the whole of the area now known as Holland Park was being built up, and soon afterwards the house and its park of 67 acres would be a green oasis between genteel Kensington and sprawling Shepherd's Bush.

years old. 'My *mere* family accounts to 25 in town now, and a *few* old friends make up beyond thirty; so that as all see my sister, and our house is a nutshell, my own family within being with myself ten at dinner, you see *I may be hurried* without what is called *seeing anybody*.'

Caroline was similarly forthright in her declaration that the capital was bad for one's health, believing as she did that London's evenings of pleasure and mornings in bed were best avoided. 'Early hours, particularly in a morning, are certainly the best remedy for bad nerves', she wrote in 1762, adding, 'I wonder

when I'm up and dressed before seven ... that I don't always do it; the custom of lying a-bed all morning, as many people do, is really losing half the enjoyment of life.'

By taking the lease of Holland House in 1749, Caroline hoped that she and Henry could combine the virtues of the country with the pleasures of the town. For Holland House, even then, was really a country house within the boundaries of London. With market gardens and gravel pits beyond the Acton Road at the northern edge of the park, and fields to the east between the Holland House gardens and the grounds of Kensington House, it felt as if the country was all around. But Caroline and Henry could drive to the West End and back comfortably in a morning, and most of their dinner guests went back home to bed in the evening. London was already lapping at the Foxes' backwater when they moved in, and a few decades later had begun to move around and beyond it. From the very beginning Caroline was fond of complaining that she was overrun with company. 'Holland House is one of the finest, most agreeable places in the world both within doors and without … a sweet place to be sure, with pretty loitering and sauntering about, great pleasure in my plants and flowers, but even that I can seldom enjoy for a whole morning without interruption.'

When Henry and Caroline moved into it, Holland House was indeed 'fine', although it was also old-fashioned and seriously dilapidated. The great mansion was begun in 1607 by a successful servant of James I, Sir Walter Cope. Cope's heiress and daughter married Sir Henry Rich, who went on to become 1st Earl of Holland and to give his name to the house. More building in the 1620s and '30s gave the house the almost fantastic turreted, terraced and cloistered look it had in Caroline's day. But it was never lived in by its owners for very long after the reign of Charles I. The Earl of Holland supported the King in the Civil War and paid for

his loyalty with his head in Palace Yard, Westminster in 1649. The house then passed laterally into the family of the Earls of Warwick, thence garnering an association that Caroline relished. In 1716, Charlotte, widow of the 5th Earl of Warwick, married the essayist and poet Thomas Addison and they went to live at Holland House. Credited with introducing and developing the notion and importance of the arts of conversation and politeness in the *Spectator* magazine, Addison was, with Shaftesbury, one of

BELOW

Meissen snuffbox with a miniature of Caroline inside the lid. This luxurious bauble was a present from Henry Fox to the 2nd Duchess of Richmond when the Foxes were reconciled with Caroline's parents in 1748. It did little to thaw the coldness between them.

the most important influences on gentlemanly manners before the fashion for French *philosophes*, domesticity and sensibility. He was one of Caroline's favourite authors, although, so familiar was the *Spectator* to her, that she knew it by heart and confessed to soporific boredom when it was read aloud as a gesture of anglophilia at a French country-house party in the early 1760s.

For all his reputation as a genial and bonhomous man, Addison did not get on with the Countess of Warwick. Their marriage was not a success. As one observer put it, 'Holland House, although a large house, could not contain Mr Addison, the Countess of Warwick, and one guest, Peace'. Addison died there in 1719, officially of asthma and dropsy, although Horace Walpole more tartly diagnosed that, 'unluckily he died of brandy'. But his association with the house was not forgotten. Over a century later, when parcels of the land around the house were being sold off for development, several streets in the new middle-class housing area that bordered the park on its western edge were named after him.

When Henry and Caroline moved into Holland House in 1749, little had changed either inside or out. Sometime in the early 1620s or '30s the architect Inigo Jones had modified parts of the interior in the classical style he had introduced from Italy, and he had also constructed two classical porches or piers to support a gate that served as an entrance to a part of the park called the Pleasure Grounds. But for the most part the original Jacobean structure and its later additions remained unaltered. Inside the house boasted room after room of heavy oak carved panelling and wainscoting and pendulous wooden or plaster coffered ceilings. By 1750, when the classical style with its emphasis on natural light, soaring and pillared spaces and much lighter (though often parti-coloured) plasterwork had swept everything before it, both interior and exterior were hopelessly old-fashioned, the more so since the age prized novelty in everything. Old-fashioned was unfashionable, especially for an aspiring politician who wanted to demonstrate his ambition and acumen.

The Foxes did not, as many must have expected, open up the interior, strip out the panelling, or remodel the whole in the classical style. They did not buy the house outright until 1767 and may have been unwilling to invest too much money in a building on a 100-year lease. Moreover, in their early years, they did not have money for major building works. But most important, Caroline loved Holland House the way it was, 'comfortable' and 'old-fashioned'.

What went on in Holland House, then, was planting and redecorating. Early on it was the park, the house's most obvious asset, that took most of the Foxes' attention. Writing to the

naturalist Peter Collinson, who was an early adviser to the rich on planting patterns and new varieties, Fox declared in 1750, 'If you will permit us, Lady Caroline has a thousand questions to ask you about flowers, and I not much fewer about plants'. Like many an amateur, Fox was eager to display a modicum of knowledge to this expert, writing with a flourish in December of the same year, 'Dear Sir … I want to raise a quantity of male spreading cypress and other cypress from seed. Can you procure me any cones? I want likewise some acorns of scarlet oak, and a bushel or more of chestnuts for sowing.' But soon this veneer of expertise crumbled. A few months later he wrote with a helpless confession of ignorance, 'Mr. Watson advis'd me to sow something with a hard name to creep on the ground and cover with green all the vacant spaces in my young plantations. I wish you would tell me what it was.' On this letter, which made its way back to Holland House, Collinson had written his reply

ABOVE

Holland House, a nineteenth-century lithograph by Day & Son showing figures on the steps and terrace dressed in costumes from 'The Olden Time', which Holland House, in its magnificent survival, had by then come to represent.

Lady Sarah Lennox by Francis Coates, 1760. Sixteen years later she described herself, with characteristic exaggeration, as, 'a thin, pale, long-nosed, hollowed-eyed, coarse-featured woman', with, 'a poking figure and negligence of dress', but everyone agreed on her startling attractiveness as a young woman.

and some notes: 'Double snowdrops. To remind him in March to sow Candy Tuft, Rock Stock, Venus Looking-Glass etc.'

Planting of this sort held little interest for either Henry or Caroline. Despite her early questions about flowers, Caroline's passion was

for greenery, especially trees. In the 1750s and '60s when any exposure to the sun was regarded as both unhealthy and socially unacceptable and when women of a certain sort put lead oxide on their faces to whiten their skin, flower gardens had few attractions unless they were edged by

Henry Lord Holland
nat: 1705. ob: 1774
Sr J. Reynolds pinx.^t

LEFT

Henry Fox, 1st Lord Holland, painted at the height of his political power by Sir Joshua Reynolds in 1762. An unscrupulous man of enormous charm, he had an eye for the ladies, and, especially for Sarah, whom he described as 'prettier than and different from any girl I ever saw'.

dry, shady gravel walks for exercise or could be viewed from above as a formal and pleasing arrangement. The more naturalistic, even 'wild' flower gardens of the 1770s came too late for Caroline, although Emily was to become a connoisseur of their planting. Flowers at Holland House seem to have been limited to hot-house specimens, spring planting under trees and perhaps a formal rose garden. Caroline's particular hobby was a greenhouse on the roof of the interior cloister of Holland House, facing west outside her first-floor rooms. 'I have got a little snug greenhouse upon my leads of each side of my dressing room window', she wrote to Emily in October 1758. 'It looks vastly pretty to have the greens so close to one. My tuberoses that I bought when I sent you yours are now in full bloom.'

But trees, especially exotic imports, had pride of place at Holland House. In her first decade of residence, Caroline mentioned to Emily that they had planted tulip trees, 'scarlet oaks', Norway maples and acacias. Emily did not share her sister's arboreal enthusiasms. 'I have asked you forty times and you won't answer me, don't you delight in scarlet oaks?', Caroline wrote in mock exasperation in 1759. 'Is it not charming to sit under shade of one's own planting? I'm fonder of plants and trees than ever I can rightly take to flowers. I love them excessively, particularly the spring ones, but I can't mind 'em enough to have 'em in great perfection; I should like a gardener that could.'

Early work inside Holland House was confined to two major projects, beyond simply making the house habitable. A room with an Inigo Jones ceiling, perhaps not originally a chapel, was restored for that purpose; and a picture gallery was created out of the original Jacobean long gallery in the west wing. Sketches of the picture gallery in the nineteenth century — when it had become the house's main library — show that although Caroline put her personal coat of arms above the door frames, and may have installed new fireplaces, she left the original carved oak cornice, the mullioned bay window at the north end and the original oak ceiling with its seven vaulted and panelled compartments.

In 1763 Caroline returned from an extended trip to Paris with a sizeable collection of French porcelain and furniture and with her Francophilia confirmed and extended to the curves, gilt, inlays and ormolu of Louis XV interior decoration. Temporarily casting off the informality of so-called 'India-paper rooms' which used hand-painted Chinese paper to cover walls, she splashed out on a grand French scheme in her drawing-room in 1764, dubbing it a 'salon' and filling it with her Paris purchases. 'I am out of conceit with Indian paper', she told Emily, 'and am all for the magnificent style — velvet, damask etc. I have three immense looking-glasses to put in my drawing room, and propose hanging it with a damask or brocatelle of two or three colours. I am rather changeable in these things, but 'tho whims and fripperies may have a run, one always returns to what is handsome and noble and plain. My glasses are to have no frame but a gilt moulding; the room is gilt, and I shall have a fine commode and two quoins I already brought from France.'

Generous in her enthusiasm for the Louis XV style, Caroline wondered if her sister Louisa, married four years before to Ireland's richest man

Joshua Reynolds's famous triple portrait of Lady Sarah Lennox, Lady Susan Fox-Strangways and the young Charles James Fox, painted for the Holland House gallery in 1764. Sarah leans down towards the others from the loggia of the west wing of Holland House, gesturing towards a bird that Susan is holding. Charles James Fox, a precocious thirteen-year-old Etonian, holds the manuscript of one of his own Latin poems.

Above

Silverware, candlesticks and glassware from the mid-eighteenth-century. Emily had a favourite glassware shop in Swallow Street in London's Mayfair, but once, having picked out some cream jars there, she forgot them, leaving her husband to pick up both the pots and the bill two years later.

and beginning to renovate the interior of his magnificent mansion of Castletown, would like an example too. She had heard that Louisa liked inlaid wood, and was eager to send something fashionable and Parisian over to Ireland. 'Pray dear siss', she wrote to Emily in 1763, 'find out for me what piece of furniture would be agreeable to Lady Louisa. I hear she likes l'Anglay's inlaid things very much and I would wish to send her something that might suit some of her rooms, whether commode table, bureau or coins, which to be sure one might vulgarly call corner cupboards; but really they are lovely and finish a room so well. I have two beauties in the salon at Holland House.'

In fact neither Emily nor Louisa shared Caroline's taste either in building or in decoration. They consulted one another, and later, Sarah, but regarded Caroline's love for the

freezing panelled spaces of Holland House as eccentric, preferring themselves classical restraint or expensive informality. All the sisters enjoyed a bit of clutter in their private rooms – porcelain jumbled on mantelpieces, books and work baskets scattered about – but that was the extent of their shared taste.

Emily's Dublin town house, Kildare House – renamed Leinster House when the Earl of Kildare became the Duke of Leinster in 1766 – was Italianate and classical in style, a world away from Holland House in its preponderance of limestone, classical columns and bas-relief plasterwork, its open spaces and straight lines. By the same token, if Caroline loved Holland House, calling herself Lady Holland after her house rather than the other way round, Emily had nothing but dislike for Leinster House. In all her long correspondence she never mentions it in terms of praise, and it was mostly associated in her mind with distress, illness, childbirth and death.

The Earl of Kildare bought the site of Leinster House for £1,000 in 1744 when he came into his inheritance, determined to build a mansion that would advertise his status as Ireland's premier peer. When taken to task for his youthful *naïveté* in proposing to build on Dublin's unfashionable south side, he declared that society would follow him wherever he went. It did; only a few years after Leinster House was built the open fields that had surrounded it were a mess of building sites and the rich were clamouring to be housed there. Fifty years later the artist James Malton described Leinster House as 'commanding a prospect few places can exhibit ... in front laid out in a spacious courtyard, the ground in the rear made a spacious lawn ... enjoying in the tumult of the noisy metropolis all the retirement of the country'.

LEFT

Monteeth for washing wine glasses, mid-eighteenth-century. The scalloped edge held the bases of the jars and prevented the delicate and expensive hand-blown glasses from banging into one another.

RIGHT
Leinster House,
Kildare Street,
Dublin. This print from
1783 shows a corps of
Volunteers patrolling
on the lawn. Always the
grandest private house
in the city, Leinster
House – originally
known as Kildare
House – eventually
became the seat of the
Irish Parliament, the
Dail.

Capel Street, Dublin, at the end of the eighteenth century. This scene, drawn by James Malton, looks south across the Liffey towards Dublin Castle, Christ Church Cathedral, where many Earls of Kildare are buried, and St Werberg's Church, where the body of Emily's son Lord Edward Fitzgerald was hastily put in the crypt in 1798.

Even by the lavish standards of contemporary Irish grand houses, Leinster House was an imposing structure. Designed by the German architect Richard Cassels, who built or worked on many of Ireland's country houses, including Powerscourt and Carton, it stood four-square, three storeys high, 70 feet deep and 140 feet long. Severely classical, it had a simple pedimented front to relieve the plainness of the grey stone façade at the front entrance on Coote Lane – which the Earl immediately renamed Kildare Street – and two shallow flights of steps up to the garden door at the back. Inside it was equally grand and simple, with stone chequered floors on the ground floor, Doric columns, marble fireplaces and a fine double staircase.

Yet Emily never liked it. So little did she care for it, indeed, that she raided it for cloth to cover furniture at her country house of Carton where she lived whenever she did not have to be in Dublin, and which to her was home. Leinster House remained a place where she played her role of 'Queen of Ireland' during the social season, and where she went, reluctantly, to lie in and endure her month of confinement after childbirth. She passed on her dislike to her children. 'What a melancholy house it is', wrote her son Lord Edward Fitzgerald to her in 1794

when he brought his wife up from the country to have her first child. 'You can't conceive how much it appeared so when first we came from Kildare. A poor country house maid I brought with me cried for two days, and said she thought she was in prison.'

The most arduous tasks, in Dublin or in London, were the innumerable public appearances that the sisters' social and political duties demanded. Going to Court in London, or to the Lord Lieutenant's shadow Court at Dublin Castle could very often be avoided, although not if there were young people who had to be presented. A certain number of assemblies and balls were also inescapable. Pleasure gardens, the theatre, masquerades and the opera made up the social round, and for all these events and occasions the sisters and their families had to be dressed correctly, and that, at least until old age allowed them licence, meant being dressed in the latest fashions. Thus fashion, although for some it was a passion, was also a duty. Following changes in stuffs and jewellery was a declaration of wealth and social standing, while an interest in new styles indicated a necessary commitment to change, novelty and progress. An old-fashioned woman, unless she was past a certain age, signalled a lack of

ABOVE

The Rotunda Hospital, Dublin, a favourite charity with the rich. Aristocratic women were expected to make charitable contributions. Emily once hit on the idea of a home for reformed prostitutes, but her husband, with more general knowledge of the subject, suggested that it wouldn't work since women of the town who gave up their jobs simply went back to their families.

ambition as well as poor credit with mercers, milliners and dressmakers. No-one, not even children, were immune to fashion's call. In 1766, Lord Henry Fitzgerald, then aged five, was proud to have his hair curled and his mother was happy to let him, as Louisa reported to Sarah from Carton House. 'That monkey Henry has just come into the room with his hair in papers. He is such a little coxcomb as never was, and gives his love to you … He now prates so I can hardly write, and routs the inkstand.'

Of the Lennox sisters, only Louisa was genuinely modest about her looks. Despite being regarded as having a fine figure if not a particularly pretty face, she constantly down-

played her own good looks, hastening to report to Emily a conversation she had had with the famous beauty the Countess of Coventry when she first arrived in London in 1759. 'I must tell you of a thing which I'm sure will divert you, and that is that Lady Coventry says she was vastly uneasy till she saw me, for fear I should be too handsome; but that when she saw me she lifted up her hands and eyes to heaven and says, "well, thank God! She is not near so handsome as Lady Kildare".'

In the first decade of her marriage, Louisa was as finely dressed as any of her sisters and acquaintances. But as time went on, she made fewer public appearances and fewer trips to London or Dublin, and with the exception of the odd masquerade or necessary visit to Court, avoided the grandest social occasions. Gradually, people began to notice that she had stopped wearing fashionable clothes, and, as she moved into middle age, noticed the increasing simplicity of her dress with something like disapprobation. While none of her sisters criticized the grey and brown outfits she took to wearing at Castletown, with their special long pockets for carrots and odd potatoes, their letters radiated a mild disapproval that was social rather than personal.

In the early years of her marriage, though, Louisa, like her sisters, enjoyed the excitement of the hunt for new and beautiful fashions and the

BELOW
Louisa – Anne-Marie Duff – and Sarah – Jodhi May – exchange confidences at Court. Louisa was regarded as the least pretty of the sisters in London, but the most beautiful in Paris, where compliments melted her habitual public shyness and she surprised even herself with her chattiness.

race to be the first to wear the latest French designs. Caroline may have scorned the idea of fashionability, and sometimes frowned upon fashions she regarded as vulgar, but nowhere in her letters does she play down the need to dress up for grand occasions. Emily and Sarah were unashamed and determined followers of fashion, and Sarah, in particular, excelled at writing about them and whipping up excitement and desire in her correspondents. As soon as she arrived in London from Ireland at the age of 14 in 1759, Sarah began closely to observe the most fashionable women and to patrol the dressmakers' studios in search of the new and rare. She was soon writing invitingly to Emily, 'I

wish you would give me a general order to buy every fashionable thing I see, for I long to get every fashionable thing for you, and am afraid'.

Scarcity, Sarah knew, was as much prized as innovation, and generally accompanied it. 'I forgot to tell you', she wrote at the end of one of her first letters from London, 'there is a sweet water tabby at Wheatly made by Lady Harrington's direction; its purple with white flowers. Do have it – it will cost but twelve guineas, which I gave for a blue and white one not half so pretty. They are vastly the fashion. Do have it before its grown common. There are but two of them sold as yet, and it will become you excessively.' Emily hardly needed encouraging.

RIGHT
Caroline – Serena Gordon – takes laudanum in the company of her sister Sarah – Jodie May – before meeting Emily after their fierce quarrel and long separation between 1769 and 1774. By the time they were reunited Emily's husband was dead and both Caroline and Lord Holland were dying.

The basic elements of a gentlewoman's gown changed little from about 1730, when the 'sack' or mantua became widespread, until about 1780, when the 'Polonaise' gown swept away the fashions of the previous fifty years. Formal gowns came in three parts: a petticoat, often with a series of under-petticoats that sat on rigid hoops or panniers to make the skirt stand out; a stomacher worn over a tight corset; and a relatively loose top-petticoat that might be nipped in at the waist or might fall in pleats from the neck and shoulders. Underneath the whole arrangement women wore a chemise – but no knickers – on to which the lace ruffles that hung below the gown's sleeves were sewn. What changed year by year were the details: the types and patterns of cloth, the silhouette, the shape of the skirt, the number and depth of the ruffles, the necklines, lace trims, hair styles, jewellery, ribbons, rouges and patches. Sometimes the very elements of the gown changed too. In the 1760s, in acknowledgement of their heaviness and unpopularity, it became fashionable to leave out the hoop from the petticoat, allowing the skirt to fall right to the ground. 'Nobody wears the little hoops here,' Caroline announced to Emily in February of that year. 'I admire the fashion of going quite without a hoop, and did from the first of all things; people look infinitely genteeler in my eyes.'

Complete formal ensembles, and completely

new outfits were worn only on important occasions. At home, in the mornings and in the country, everyone muddled along, mixing stomachers, top-gowns and different styles and fabrics, wearing comfortable quilted petticoats in the winter and going without constricting and cumbersome hoops and panniers. They often wore négligés, in which the bodice and skirt, although still fitted, were cut and sewn as one, making the whole outfit easy and quick to put on. Very loose over-gowns, like comfortable house-coats, could be thrown over everything and pulled around one in cold corridors and draughty rooms. Married women who were almost continuously pregnant, like Emily, had bodices that could be loosened at the sides so that they could be comfortable and healthy in the last six months of pregnancy. As always moreover, everyone had their favourite garments, that defied fashionable taste and stayed in the wardrobe long after their day was done; these, too, could be worn in the mornings and at home.

High fashion, then, was never continuously worn, even by the grandest and the worst smitten. But it was still a demanding taskmistress. To be sure of catching the latest styles, women had to scour the newspapers, listen to gossip and tour the mercers and milliners for the latest ribbons, caps, lace, feathers and false flowers. Londoners were plagued with commissions by those behindhand

LEFT

Triple lace ruffles like those shown here would be tacked to the 'blonde', or white cotton shift that was worn under the stomacher and petticoat. Since lace was very expensive, ladies maids would transfer the ruffles from one suit of blonde to another. ABOVE Girls such as Emily, played by Geraldine Somerville, would wear simple versions of adult clothing.

FAR LEFT
Details of gentlemen's coats from the 1770s – and LEFT from the 1780s. For the *Aristocrats* series, material for coats and waistcoats was bought in London. The made-up garments were flown with pattern designs and embroidery silk to Pakistan, where they were embroidered by skilled craftsmen in a matter of days and flown back to London.

with the fashion. 'My dearest Sarah', wrote Louisa in 1761, when she was still only 18 years old, 'I should be vastly obliged to you if you would be so good as to execute the commissions I am going to tell you for me. ... I beg you will be so good as to get me 6 yards of black velvet ribbon of every different size, and three dozen yards of lilac ribbon, one dozen of narrow and two of broad, and also two dozen yards of large pink ribbon, and two dozen yards of narrow of the same sort. I beg you will also send me a dozen of fine large chip hats, and that you will get all these things immediately; ... you know how impatient one is to get everything in a minute. ... I have two thousand things to get over, but I don't think of them now ... Send me also from Mrs Labord as many yards of blonde as is necessary to make treble ruffles and to go round a large robing handkerchief; it must cost but 0:8s:0d a yard, I know she has some lovely blonde at that price. ... Pray buy me a bunch of garnets enough to make bracelets with twelve rows — let them be large.'

The richest, and the most influential, could make shopkeepers and dressmakers come to them, but when they succumbed to temptation it would inevitably hit their pockets hard: fashion, to be fashionable, had to be expensive too. 'By the by', wrote Sarah to Emily in 1759, 'a woman brought me some Japanese mousseline to see. Its very dear, so I did not take it; but I think it so pretty that I got a bit to show you. If you will have some, send word immediately, for she has very little, and 'twill be bought up immediately, and you know one can't get it over again. This was a price, I think its eighteen shillings a yard,

and a yard wide . . . its all over with little flowers.' Since a gown with petticoat and stomacher would take at least fifteen yards, the cloth alone for a new outfit would cost almost £15, nearly twice the annual wage of a Carton House maid. And the cloth was only the beginning — the cost would rocket when the gown had been made up and trimmed with rouching or ribbons or lace.

Luckily for Emily, this sort of expense did not bother the Earl of Kildare. On the contrary it excited him and he felt that it was Emily's due as his wife and as a beautiful woman. Besides, running an expenditure in excess of his income was a way of life only partly explained by Emily's

RIGHT

A cotton Polonaise from the 1770s. The Polonaise, with its shortened petticoat and milkmaid look, became extremely widespread in the 1780s and swept away the looser-fitting gowns of the previous half century. Cottons, too, became gradually universal and caused the ruin of many prosperous silk merchants.

extravagance. Set alongside paying £3,000 annually for his widowed mother, the expense of a large family and the ruinously costly alterations at Carton House, Emily's demands seemed only intermittently excessive. Kildare was as eager a consumer as his wife, as he explained excitedly in a letter from London in May 1759: 'This day my dear Emily's gown was given to Mrs Labord to be made up; which I flatter myself she will like, for then I shall be pleased in having made choice of a silk both to her taste and mine. It is not a silk of last year's, but one of the first made for the next winter. I will not tell you what sort it is, but it is what you will look handsomer by far in than anybody else would, that I have yet seen in England.'

Coiffures were as extravagant as gowns and could also be extremely expensive, demanding pads of false hair, yards of ribbon and skeins of pearls and other jewels. So complicated that they were often left in place for weeks, coiffures were ideal breeding grounds for lice, hence the heavy use of powder that was supposed to discourage them. From the 1760s, however, powdering gradually became less prevalent. Jacques Casanova, on his London sojourn of 1764, noticed Sarah Lennox's Suffolk neighbour Lady Grafton at a London ball with her unpowdered hair curling loosely about her shoulders. But this was still the equivalent of 'undress', as Sarah herself explained in a letter to

Susan Fox-Strangways two years later, in which she distinguished between an everyday style and something 'perfectly genteel' that could be seen in a drawing-room. 'I have cut off my hair', she wrote, 'and find it very convenient in the country without powder because my hair curls naturally, but its horrid troublesome to have it well curled;

ABOVE

Silk waistcoat from the 1780s. At the end of filming series like *Aristocrats*, costumes are usually sold, sometimes to the actors themselves but more often to professional costumiers.

if its big, its frightful. ...To be perfectly genteel you must be dressed thus. Your hair need not be cut off, for its much too pretty, but it must be powdered, curled in very small curls, and ... it must be high before and give your head the look of a sugar loaf a little. The roots of your hair must be drawn up straight, & not frizzed at all for half an inch above the root.'

Sarah was accepted as an authority on fashionable coiffures by her sisters, but the last word went to hairdressers who were already masters of petty tyranny in the interests of fashion and profit. When Louisa Conolly arrived in London for a visit in the spring of 1768, she found instructions from Sarah about where she should have her hair done waiting for her. 'I found your two notes here and have obeyed your commands about Le Blanc the hairdresser, for I let him dress me just as he thought proper. I hope I was dressed like an Angel, but I am no judge, as it is not the manner I am used to. He put an immense cushion of horse hair on my head to support my cap, which he said you always wore, and my hair was dressed like yours.'

Emily's great weakness — or perhaps it was really Kildare's — was not so much her head as her feet. She had, according to her devoted husband, 'sweet' and 'pretty' legs and she was fond of expensive stockings to set them off. She particularly favoured stockings that had been 'clocked', or stretched and embroidered above the ankle on the outside of the leg. Although the origin of the term was obscure — perhaps coming from a similarity between the shape of the embroidered section and that of a clock pendulum — the effect of the procedure was not. Clocks invited the eye to travel up the leg from the ankle and winked out invitingly from under women's petticoats. Emily loved them and asked for a number of pairs when Kildare went to London in 1762. His generosity exceeded even her extravagance, however, as he explained excitedly. 'I find I exceeded your commission in regard to your stockings with colour'd clocks. I bespoke two pairs with bright blue, two pairs with green, and two pairs with pink coloured clocks, all different patterns, and will wash very well, as Barker informs me. I hope you will not dislike them; I am sure when you have them on, your dear legs will set them off. I will bespoke you six more pairs with white clocks; you mean to have them embroidered, I suppose, therefore I shall order them so and make you a present of the dozen. The writing about your stockings and dear, pretty legs makes me feel what is not to be expressed, tho' I want nothing to remind me of my lovely Emily, for she is always present to whereso'er I go. I would give ten worlds to be an hour with you my dearest Angel, for life to me is nothing without you.' Emily did have to pay for her finery, of course. 'I ... long very much for the acknowledgement [your] dear, dear legs are

LEFT

George III in coronation robes, studio of Allan Ramsay. One of literally scores of copies of Ramsay's coronation portrait which are still to be found in many country houses. Ramsay also painted Queen Charlotte, but her portrait was copied much less frequently, perhaps because she was regarded as quite exceptionally plain.

ABOVE

A painted fan from the mid-eighteenth century. In England fans were used exclusively by women, but in Italy, Emily's son William observed men – even priests, he reported with some astonishment – fanning themselves in the streets and bought himself one in Florence with which to fan himself to sleep in the heat of the summer.

to make me for the trouble I have had upon their account, and make no doubt but that I shall be amply rewarded for the care I have had about them. My expectation this day has been so raised by what you say for them that I doubt I shall sleep but little tonight for thinking of them.'

Kildare's trips to London, ostensibly on political business, often turned into giant spending sprees, and Emily was usually their beneficiary. While at home he attempted to control his expenditure, away from Emily Kildare gave up the pretence and indulged to the full the connection he made between sexual desire and spending money. He missed her horribly and freely admitted it. After seeing their eldest two boys in London in 1762, he wrote to her sadly, 'Our boys are very well, and I have nothing to add but that my absence from my dearest

Emily I look upon as so much of my life lost, as I find I cannot enjoy life without you are with me.' In this melancholy mood, buying things for Emily came easily, and London's retailers put nothing in his way. Indeed, by the mid-eighteenth century London was famous throughout Europe for the number and variety of its shops and for the crowds of people strolling about looking and buying from eight in the morning until darkness and beyond. Although specialist trades were still concentrated in particular areas of the city – printers in St Paul's Churchyard, booksellers in St James's and the Strand, for instance – the West End was fast becoming a teeming temple to consumption. In 1786, Sophie de la Roche, visiting from Frankfurt, described walking the length of Oxford Street by lamplight: 'We strolled up and down lovely Oxford Street this evening, for some goods look more attractive by artificial light. Just imagine … a street taking half an hour to cover from end to end with double rows of brightly shining lamps … The pavement, inlaid with flagstones, can stand six people deep and allow one to gaze at the splendidly lit shop fronts in comfort. First one passes a watchmakers, then a silk or fan store, now a silversmith's, a china or glass shop. Just as alluring are the confectioners and fruiterers, where, behind the handsome glass windows, pyramids of pineapples, figs, grapes, oranges and all manner of fruits are on show. Up to eleven o'clock at night there are as many people along this street as at Frankfurt during the fair, not to mention the constant stream of coaches.'

While there were many commentators ready to deplore London's affair with Mammon, Kildare was not among them. He was entirely free of guilt about spending money, regretting only that he did not have more of it. On his 1759 trip to London, besides the sumptuous silk gown, he bought two 'suits of blonde', or

BELOW
Silver sweetmeat baskets from the 1750s. It was in this decade that Emily, embarking on the refurbishment of Carton House, made bulk purchases of luxury goods that she regarded as necessities, and she was more than capable of ordering this sort of thing by the dozen.

RIGHT AND FAR RIGHT
Irish ash and peat
buckets and an Irish
walnut wing chair.
Louisa and Emily
burned coal in their
houses, but amongst the
rich, peat burning
became a fashionable
declaration of
patriotism towards the
end of the century.
Emily's son, Lord
Edward Fitzgerald,
burned peat, drank
Irish whiskey and
danced Irish jigs to
Irish pipes to
demonstrate his
revolutionary zeal at the
end of the century.

sets of undergarments for Emily, a quantity of ribbons and bows, 150 yards of painted taffeta to hang on the walls of Carton's state rooms, several miniatures, two bottles of special medicine and a number of books. He looked out and sent off to Ireland various sheets of Chinese wallpaper – or 'India paper', as it was called – to furnish Emily's downstairs parlour and also found time to have his own carriage repaired and repainted– all this in six weeks. 'I am really so loaded with things, not only for you but others, that I don't know what to do, or how I shall get them ashore in Ireland', he wrote almost boastfully, and added, 'I have perform'd all the commissions that belong to you. As to pictures, tables, brooches, they have not been enquired after yet, and I am afraid to look for them, they will cost so much, and this year I fear will be my ruin.' In the middle of this extended shopping trip he did once panic, pleading with Emily to lessen her demands. 'My love, my love, it is very great pleasure to write for things to be sent to one; but the paying is not so when it is inconvenient ... I am extremely

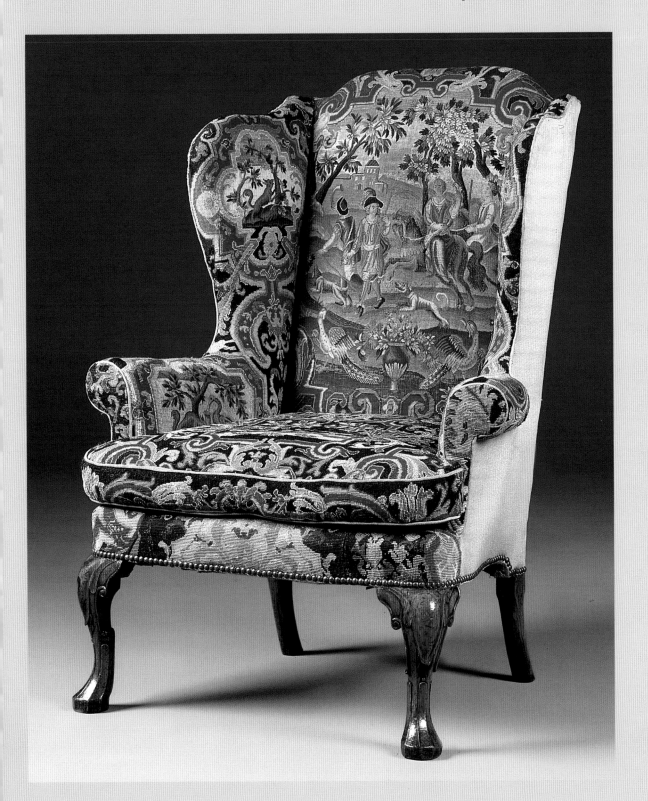

ABOVE

Tom Conolly – Tom Mullion – and his bride Louisa – Anne-Marie Duff – steal a kiss after their wedding ceremony in 1759. Their marriage seemed to Louisa to be a success in every way. She did not discover until after Tom died that he had for many years kept a mistress in Leixlip, a few miles from Castletown. The revelation devastated her, but she refused to blame him, saying only that he would answer to God for his actions.

concerned to send such a letter as this to my dearest Emily, but she will I hope take it as a hint, and not as a lecture for what is passed.' But even this mild rebuke was beyond him, and a few lines later he qualified it, saying, 'I long much to have one of my Emily's dear kisses; tho' the first part of my letter may have the appearance of not caring for them much, yet be assured I did not feel to love you less than I have done when I wrote before.' The Earl of Kildare continued to be a slave to his desire for his wife and, besides, he was every bit as committed to extravagance as she. Wisely, Emily never tempered her demands, only once going so far as to write –

though without a hint of remorse or a promise of better behaviour – 'I am quite shocked at the thoughts of my Jemmy's having such sums all at once to pay for his extravagant wife.'

Kildare's 1759 trip took place at the beginning of a surge in the fortunes of the wealthy and of the middle classes who depended upon them. This prosperity reached its height during the 1760s and only levelled off as confidence drained away during the long and ignominious American wars.

The boom years began during the Seven Years War of 1756–63. Huge fortunes were made during the war, some by financiers or government ministers like Henry Fox, others by army and navy suppliers. Boots, biscuits, beef, weaponry, ships – all had to be ordered, made and delivered. But slaughter was itself a profitable trade. Army agents who conscripted troops could do very nicely, and many shared in prize money on the field or at sea. The Seven Years War was fought in the Americas, the Mediterranean and the East Indies, where the East India Company wiped out the French interest in the sub-continent. While the British

Crown paid for others to do most of the land-based fighting – with the taking of Canada a memorable exception – there were plenty of British ships in action on the seas. Victories brought not only new colonies, like Canada, and new markets, like the East Indies, but also scores of immediately tangible assets – ships and their cargoes. Prize money – a proportion of the value of the booty – was apportioned like a profit share according to the sailor's place in the capturing ship's hierarchy of command. Everybody got something. A really valuable haul

BELOW

Sarah – Jodhi May – and Susan – Pauline McLynn – share a word at a banquet. Sarah is wearing a sack gown, wide hoops and deep ruffles, all fashionable accoutrements of the 1760s.

could allow a captain to retire in style and a midshipman to open a small business or shop when the war ended and he came home. It was thus not only the fighting men who were enriched, but the wider economy.

For as long as the war lasted, farmers and all concerned with agriculture also did well, although rents and wages would fall off immediately peace was declared. War guaranteed high prices for produce that was needed to feed troops, and that meant high rents for landlords, prosperity for tenant farmers and work for agricultural labourers. The agricultural economy in Ireland, which was a convenient way-station on the journey to the West Indies, boomed as a result, although there was always subsistence farming and great poverty there. The Irish economy, moreover, was no small economy: Ireland had a population of 8 million, two-thirds the size of the population of England and Wales by the end of the century.

As Irish opposition politicians, the Earl of Kildare prominent among them, complained, by no means all of this money stayed in the country. Prosperity meant that the Irish treasury ran a surplus, and it was cheerfully bagged by Westminster. A great deal more money came out into the hands of absentee landlords. Even men like Tom Conolly and the Duke of Leinster, who lived in Ireland, went to London to shop for luxury goods. Decades before it supplied the

manpower to kick-start the Industrial Revolution, Ireland fed the British economy a constant shower of golden nectar.

By the time the war ended in 1763, the rich had already indulged in several years of rampant consumerism. Despite widespread short-term unemployment caused by returning troops flooding the labour market and the ending of government contracts, and despite the agricultural depression that followed the peace, they did not stop spending. Moreover, the lucky troops and sailors who came home with money, invested it in the local economy and went some way to balancing the hardship peace created. Money from new territories in India soon began to pour in; nabobs were made. The reopening of links with the Continent allowed the import of luxury goods again. Thousands who had been deprived of French fashions and salons and Italian art and antiques, rushed abroad and loaded up with clothes, porcelain, statues and paintings.

Travellers arriving in London after the end of the war noticed the frenzy of consumption with astonishment: the building of rows of classical town houses, the variety and glitter of the shops, the vibrant print culture and the political opposition that it fed. They marvelled at the eagerness with which the rich embraced novelty and changing fashion, passing their old outfits to servants so that visitors were confused by the grandeur of their dress. Huge fortunes were dissipated in card playing, horse racing and building spectacular new country houses.

Although Britain continued to be more prosperous and more expensive than her European neighbours for several decades, the American war altered the national mood. In the first place Britain lost the war and with it a captive market. In the second place it was not a war that generated huge amounts of money. It was a land-based, slow-burning, guerrilla war, which produced few prisoners and few prizes.

Returning soldiers did not bring booty, they brought tales of incompetence and sickness. By the time the war was over in 1781, confidence had dropped. The 1780s did not see an end to extravagance – far from it – but a slightly reckless mood accompanied big-spending that was a far cry from the breezy confidence of the 1760s.

Although shopping may have been the London activity closest to Emily's heart, it came second in the eyes of the world to the duties of attending to social and political business. The most

BELOW
The 2nd Duke and Duchess of Richmond sit through a concert with their children. Although the 3rd Duke of Richmond enjoyed music and patronized the opera, none of his sisters showed very much interest in it.

important London duties and, sometimes, pleasures, for those who lived there and those who visited, were attendance at Court, at assemblies and balls where political alliances were forged and cemented and at drums, masquerades and pleasure gardens where gossip was exchanged and marriages might be arranged.

The first thing that had to be got out of the way at the beginning of the Season or the start of a visit was a trip to St James's. Aristocrats who arrived in London had to go to Court as soon as they could so as not to be seen to be delaying their respects to the King; this was particularly important for a man like the Earl of Kildare who was a figurehead in his own country for opposition to the King's government. 'I kiss'd the King's hand today', the Earl of Kildare reported to Emily the day after he arrived in London in 1759. 'I think he looks just as he did, but less colour, and one eye gone. I cannot be presented to any more of the Royal Family till next Thursday, which is a great disappointment to me, for I hoped to have had all over by the next Drawing Room.'

Everyone agreed that the Court of the elderly George II was a dull place. Besides, as the children of courtiers, the Lennox sisters had few illusions about majesty. None the less when the King died in 1760, even they felt a surge of interest in his heir, in the glamour of a young and vigorous Court, the excitement of a coronation and the inevitability of a royal wedding.

For nearly a year before his father's death, the Prince of Wales, now George III, had been paying marked attention to Sarah Lennox. Sarah had been sent over from Ireland when she was only 15 to capture a husband whose wealth and prospects would be equal to her beauty and connections. Sarah won the devotion and ardour of the Prince, but not his hand. In May 1761 it was announced that he was to marry the 17-year-old Princess Charlotte of Mecklenburg-Strelitz.

Partly because they felt slighted on Sarah's behalf, the Lennox sisters showed more interest in the King's wedding and coronation than they were subsequently to do in any royal event. In the first place, they rejoiced that Princess Charlotte was not just plain but obviously ugly. Even Allan Ramsay, who made his name and fortune with the official Court portraits of the King and Queen that were copied for innumerable drawing-rooms in the next few years, could not disguise her looks. 'I shall like to know how [the King] looks when Miss Charlotte arrives', Louisa Conolly wrote to Sarah from Ireland on 30 July 1761. 'I hear she has an ugly nose and a wide mouth and is fair.'

When the Princess did arrive, however, even jaded aristocrats and jealous sisters were swept up in the national excitement. 'Only think',

LEFT
George III – Luke de Lacy – in his coronation robes. For the TV series, costume designer James Keast used his extensive knowledge of contemporary portraits, and especially of the work of Allan Ramsay, to great effect. Luke de Lacy's costume was taken directly from Ramsay's coronation portrait, and several of the sisters' gowns were taken from their own portraits. Costumes were made up almost exactly as they were in the sisters' day, and, for the ever-pregnant Emily, there was even a stomacher with ties at the side that could be loosened as her screen pregnancies progressed. James Keast designed everything up to the chin; above was the work of make-up and hair specialists and wig designer Lesley Lamont-Fisher.

ABOVE

ABOVE

George III receiving visitors at Court. When aristocrats arrived in London, it was customary and necessary for those with political duties and ambitions to kiss the hand of the King and of other senior members of the Royal family, a task many regarded as tedious in the extreme, before embarking on other public duties.

Emily wrote to her husband on 8 September 1761, 'how unlucky I was to come to Lady Harrington's just 10 minutes too late to see the first meeting between the King and Queen. The coach drove through the park, stopped at the garden door, which the King opened himself. She threw herself at his feet; he raised her up, embrac'd her and led her thro' the garden up the steps into the Palace. All this they saw from Lady Harrington's wall as plain as possible.'

Most of the time, however, there was more duty than romance attached to Court life. The Earl of Kildare waited two weeks to be able to report in 1759 that he had kissed the requisite number of royal hands. 'I missed writing to you last Thursday, as I was in a great hurry all day; for I kissed the Prince of Wales's hand, the Princess of Wales's, Prince Edward's and Princess Augusta's', he was finally able to write. After that, there were still a number of calls to be made on family, friends and political acquaintances. After his final duties had been fulfilled at Court, Kildare went on to his sister Lady Hillsborough for dinner, 'and went in the evening ... to Lady Harrington's to a drum, where there was a good deal of company; and after that to a ball at Mr Conolly's, where I saw Lord George Lennox and the Duchess of Richmond ... Between dinner and Lady Harrington's, I went to see Lady Essex, who sent me a message to desire I would come to see her.'

Of all the social events of the Season in both London and Dublin, balls were the most testing and important for a host and hostess. Immensely expensive displays of wealth, at which the hosts threw open their houses, poured out their wine cellars and showed off the abilities of their cooks, they none the less depended for success on the attendance and enjoyment of the guests. Though guests might come as a duty, they would only stay on if it was a pleasure. Lavishness and luxury, as well as a good guest list, were therefore vital. After reading his wife's report of a ball she gave in his absence in Leinster House in 1762,

the Earl of Kildare criticized Stoyte, his butler, for stinting on food and wine. 'I had the pleasure of my dear Emily's long letter with the account of her ball, which I was glad to find went off well, tho' Stoyte was more careful than was quite right upon such as occasion; but notwithstanding his want of judgement, I hope there was little appearance of his economy in general.'

Even Caroline, who disliked spending money on what she saw as evanescent luxury, and who admitted that she was 'apt to grudge people their victuals', was careful not to let any hint of meanness compromise the grandeur and ambition of the balls she was occasionally called upon to give at Holland House or her grand mansion in Piccadilly. Even at a smallish ball for

LEFT

George III performs his social duties in return. Although many were excited by the prospect of an invigorated and lively Court when George III succeeded his grandfather, in fact George III's court, especially when he lived domestically at Windsor, was spectacularly dull and drove many courtiers to distraction.

about seventy people that she gave in Holland House on May Day in 1753, the food was given the most careful thought. There was wine — probably burgundy and champagne — circulating during the dancing, cards and conversation, and Caroline's housekeeper, Mrs Fannen, supervised the distribution of tea and negus (a spiced sherry) in the tapestry room for those who did not drink wine. 'At one', one of the guests recorded, 'we all went down to a cold supper, at three tables in the saloon, and three in the dining room, Supper was removed at each table with a desert and ice. Sat down to supper in all sixty two. Lord Digby and Mr Bateman did not sup, but walk'd about admiring.'

The dancing at Caroline's ball took place in the gilt drawing-room, perhaps her grandest room, and on the balcony, which was especially lit for the night. It did not begin until after supper, which allowed plenty of time for the exchange of witticisms and pleasantries that she saw as proper social intercourse. There were 21 couples dancing, and none, it was recorded left before three in the morning or after five.

Besides dancing there was a good deal of card playing. Henry Fox made up a quadrille table with Caroline's aunt Lady Albemarle, his sister Mrs Digby and old Lady Yarmouth. There were nine whist players, including the Duke of Marlborough, the Duchess of Bedford — a

RIGHT

George III — Luke de Lacy — with Sarah Lennox — Jodhi May. 'She is everything I can figure to myself lovely', he confessed to his mentor Lord Bute. Despite the fact that the débâcle led eventually to Sarah's disastrous marriage to Charles Bunbury, she always maintained that she was glad that she never became queen.

woman Caroline thoroughly disliked but who was invited for political reasons – Mr Fox's protégé and confidant Mr Rigby and the witty Lady Townshend. At another table Emily played cribbage with Mrs Ellis, Lord Bury, Lord Digby and Caroline's friend Mr Bateman. Finally various guests, the observers and the unsociable, 'only look'd on'. They included Horace Walpole, Caroline's cousin Admiral Keppel and the Earl of Kildare, who, as time went on, became more and more bored by occasions where wit and sociability were called for.

Caroline's end of the Season gathering in 1753 may not have had a specific *raison d'être*, but sometimes balls had a transparent purpose. When Sarah Lennox came to London in 1759 in order to find a husband, Caroline let no opportunity slip of displaying her charms before prospective suitors. Besides taking Sarah to Ranelagh and allowing her to go to the less exclusive Vauxhall Gardens because she had heard that the eligible Duke of Marlborough was to be there, Caroline threw a ball with the purpose of throwing the couple together.

'Now for the ball', Sarah wrote to Emily happily a few days afterwards. 'We had five and twenty couples standing up for a little while, and then we divided, and went into another room, which improved it vastly… We had a long table at supper in the largest room, at the upper end of which sat the Duke of Marlborough in the middle … my sister on one side, Prince Edward by her, Lady Stanhope and others; t'other side I sat, then Lord Huntingdon, Lady Bolingbroke, Mr Fox and others. At a little table in the next room the Duchess [of Richmond] made a party, and there were three tables for the sitters by upstairs, which were not touched, there being so few. Our table was the pleasantest great table I was ever at, for they in general are terrible.'

Sarah should have been alerted to the purpose of the ball by this seating arrangement, but she was determined not to take any notice, writing only, 'My brother and sister and Mr Fox have taken it into their heads that the Duke of Marlborough liked me a little.' Caroline was more candid, telling Emily, 'My ball was pretty and went off very well. Sal seem'd much delighted. The Duke of Marlborough admires her of all things; my brother is vastly anxious to have it come to something. [The Duke] has never been known to talk so much or seem so well pleased as he did at this ball, and seem'd charmed with Sal.' Caroline's expensive entertainment did not bear fruit; two years later Sarah married Charles Bunbury; no duke, but the son of a Suffolk baronet and a much less desirable match.

At all balls, tables would be set aside for card players. Even at Caroline's ball of 1753, well before the great upsurge of gambling in the 1760s that lasted until at least the French Revolution, 18 people were sitting playing cards

in preference to dancing. Cards, and innumerable other forms of gambling from lotteries to simple bets, permeated every level of society and were to be found at most social events where people sat down. When calls were made in the evenings, card-tables came out. For people who did not like being read to and for moments when conversation ran out or when there was no music to hand, cards were the easiest way of passing the time. It was Caroline's opinion that they were 'the amusement of older age' and 'an excellent resource against ennui, ill health, bad spirits and bad eyes'. But she pronounced decisively in 1762, long before her own boys became some of the most infamous gamblers of the age, that cards were a waste of time for active, cheerful young people. Many young people did not agree. Mary Bruce, for instance, who married the 3rd Duke of Richmond in 1757, was not a woman who enjoyed reading. In London, she liked to gamble. 'I have a silver loo party for the Duchess almost every night', Emily admitted to her husband in September 1761. 'But what can one do? Cards are a necessary evil.' She did not add, though she might have, that she enjoyed cards too. They were, after all, another way of spending money.

After the establishment of Almack's gaming club in 1764, and particularly in the early years of the 1770s, gambling for very high stakes took on the quality of a mania, and was condemned in language that two hundred years later was reserved for addiction to heavy drugs. Critics maintained that young men, Caroline's sons Ste and Charles James prominent among them, seemed to be gambling not just their fortunes but their lives away, ruining their health by playing all night and compromising their futures by squandering their wealth. In the 1750s, however, gambling might have been ubiquitous, but it had not developed — in the eyes of commentators, at any rate — into a pursuit that was primarily self-destructive. Particular individuals played for high stakes and many lost large sums of money. But for most, cards offered the opportunity to sit, chat and pass the evening away. Money did constantly change hands, and most people came out net losers; Emily wrote with annoyance about losing £20 in an evening. Twenty pounds was not a negligible amount, but set against an annual income of £15,000, in Kildare's case, or £25,000 for a man like Tom Conolly, it would not have cost Emily any sleep.

Loo, which Emily played with the Duchess of Richmond, was probably the most popular card game in the aristocratic drawing-rooms of the 1750s and '60s, and kept its pre-eminent position until it was overtaken by Faro. The games played at Caroline's ball were social as well as addictive and were played at varying speeds. Quadrille, like loo, was played fast and generated a good deal of excitement in the

LEFT
Lord Kildare – Ben Daniels – and his wife Emily – Geraldine Somerville – at their wedding. A skit on their grandeur, which she sent to Henry Fox, ran in part: 'For the mimic of majesty none so fit/As Lady Kildare of Carton/The beaux they all bow when her Ladyship nods/ My Lady Kildare of Carton/Who thinks herself raised to the state of the gods/ By Lord Kildare of Carton.'

RIGHT
RIGHT
Lord Kildare – Ben Daniels – with guests at a banquet. Irish houses were famous for their hospitality; so much so, indeed, that Emily, soon after arriving there, claimed that 'everybody in Ireland spend all they have in eating and drinking and have no notion of any other sorts of comfort in life'.

players. Both games consisted in playing for tricks using trumps. In loo, players attempted to win as much of a predetermined pool as possible with their tricks, while those who failed to win tricks were obliged to increase the amount in the pool. It could become expensive because the players themselves decided on the amount in the pool and the ways in which the pool was both won and increased. Failure to take any tricks, for instance, might force a player to double the size of the pool. As the night wore on large amounts might thus be at stake. In quadrille the right to nominate trumps went to the highest bidder with the winner effectively playing against the other three hands. These players attempted to undermine the bidder by taking tricks off him, although the

bidder often had a secret partner to add a complication to the game.

Whist and cribbage were longer, more sedate and more cerebral games. Both used tricks to score points which were then translated into wins and losses. Whist was played with partners, cribbage with two players and a peg board to tot up points.

At Caroline's ball Emily chose to be seen playing cribbage, probably because her husband was present and because she was heavily pregnant and therefore not in a condition to tolerate excitement. But in more intimate parties, both preferred loo or whist. By the time Sarah became a gambler in the late 1760s, when her marriage to Sir Charles Bunbury was fast disintegrating, Faro – or Pharaoh – had become the raciest

Henry Fox was regarded as an excessively indulgent father and his son Charles James as an excessively indulged child, accustomed to attending the grandest of political dinners at Holland House even as a child. On one occasion – shown here in a still from the TV series – Charles James, played by Feargal Geraghty, was allowed to ride on top of a joint of meat with the statesmen of Europe looking on. On another he was allowed to slop about in a great bowl of cream that was to have been used for the dessert.

A printed fan, with a coloured etching on the leaf of card players, probably an allegory of diplomats negotiating the Treaty of Aix in 1748. The print culture of the day, in which prints were the vehicle of political satire as well as humour, was all-pervasive, extending to trinkets like fans and to jugs, mugs and handkerchiefs, all produced as keepsakes rather than items of use.

past-time of the fast set. Faro could be played by any number of people and was therefore particularly suitable to groups that grew and shrank through wild nights. Players placed bets with a banker on the likelihood of their cards being the same as cards that were put in a special box by the dealer. It was a risky game partly because players could bet on a number of outcomes, partly because they could choose how much to bet and partly because the banker enjoyed a built-in advantage. So, unless everyone took a turn at being the banker, players were

statistically bound to lose. Only the hot-headed and the reckless would choose to play, therefore, unless they were assured of a turn with the bank. But simply because the stakes – and thus the potential winnings – were so high, Faro had a particular attraction for the addictive and the gullible. No wonder, then, that it was at Faro that women like the Duchess of Devonshire lost huge sums of money in the late 1770s and the early 1780s.

One reason why card games were so suited to the manners of the aristocracy was that they

involved concealment and strategy, two qualities that were at the heart of metropolitan aristocratic life. Until naturalness became fashionable in the 1770s, high society valued skilful artifice in manner and behaviour extremely highly, whether it was in flirtation and wit, in false hair and face patches, in rouge and lead-white. In the theatre, a form of entertainment founded on the very idea of impersonation, it was plays of deception and mistaken identity, from *The Beaux' Stratagem* to *The Rivals*, which proved most enduringly popular. The masquerade, an act of collective impersonation, became briefly the most fashionable form of semi-public entertainment. Masquerades might be socially exclusive; some were completely private, for others tickets were sold but carefully controlled. But none the less the fun of them for participants was that, unlike a fancy-dress ball, the identity of those there was genuinely concealed, not only by their costumes but also by their masks.

Even Louisa, who was the least interested of all the Lennox sisters in the mores of metropolitan life, was tempted by the idea of anonymity that the masquerade offered. After attending a memorable, and famous, masquerade in Soho in 1770, when she was 27 years old, she wrote to Emily, 'I was never more diverted than at the masquerade; it was one of the prettiest sights I ever saw. The house at Soho is

so well calculated for it, there were 800 people, but not the least crowd. … I can't say I saw an ugly dress, and most of them so becoming… Some very ridiculous ones, which added vastly to the show; some very witty characters very well kept up: a singing Mungo, who acted very well; a mad Wilkes, very clever; some men in old women's clothes, very entertaining; and what you'll see in the papers, a double man, vastly well managed … Mr Conolly was a Spaniard. It became him of all things; he looked quite pretty. Mine was a Lady Abbess, white corded tabby, gauze and beads, a black veil, and scarlet knot to tie the diamond cross.'

One reason why concealment of this sort came as a relief and a diversion was that social life in London and, to a lesser extent, in Dublin was as much a matter of watching and being watched as it was of saying or doing anything in particular. London had a celebrity culture based around the theatre from perhaps the 1730s onwards, and in the 1760s it began to make inroads into aristocratic society. Writers, actors, naturalists, and other men of science and the odd painter mingled with peers and politicians in the drawing-room. David Garrick entertained aristocrats at his Thames-side villa and they were flattered to be invited. Beauty, too, was thrust into the limelight. Women famous simply for being beautiful, like the Irish Gunning sisters, could marry into the aristocracy. Celebrated or

Right
William O'Brien, charmer and matinée idol, by Francis Coates, about 1763. He eloped with Susan Fox-Strangways in 1763, was forced to give up the stage and, after a disastrous sojourn with her in New York, became a country gentleman. 'You was determined to fix me yours to the last period of my days and you have', he told Susan.

notorious foreigners, like the Corsican General Pasquali Paoli or the French ambassador the Chevalier d'Eon, could also draw guests to an assembly. Few aristocrats were immune to the glamour of beauty or fame. 'I was at a party Saturday night where Paoli was', Louisa reported to Emily in 1770. 'He is a fair man, and not at all answerable to the idea I had formed of him. One would never take him to be a foreigner; he looks so English and you might see him very often without taking the least notice of him . . . I hope to get acquainted with him.'

Town life was not entirely about going out and being on display. There were still quiet mornings and evenings when no visitors called and there was time for reading, 'working', gossiping, letter writing and gentle family games of cards. Writing letters was, for the most part, a

LEFT

Susan O'Brien in the companion portrait by Coates, about 1764. She was an ambitious and strong-willed woman, writing, when George III was courting her friend Sarah Lennox, 'I almost thought myself Prime Minister'. She never admitted to regretting her elopement with an actor, but grumbled perpetually about their poverty and their lack of powerful patrons.

morning activity, often done before breakfast; reading, chatting and 'working' at various kinds of embroidery were kept for the early evening, after dinner but before supper and cards.

For all the sisters except Louisa, writing letters was as much a pleasure as a duty. Louisa, although a conscientious writer whose correspondence with Sarah alone spanned almost sixty years and ran to thousands of sheets of paper, constantly tormented herself with her tardiness in replying to letters, and claimed that she disliked writing, admitting to Sarah in 1778 that she did not get carried away by writing, but on the contrary was often unnecessarily brief. 'I have no tallents for letter writing,' she wrote, 'don't love it and therefore always do curtail my subjects as much as possible.' Caroline and Sarah, on the other hand, relished telling stories that required a sustained effort with the pen. Caroline was also particularly good at responding to hints and tidbits in the letters of others, sending them back with her own thoughts and reflections, drawing her correspondents into her world as well as taking notice of theirs. In June 1759, for instance, she received a letter from Emily about a visit she had made to a house called Brockly Park. A 'sweet little place', Emily called it, and particularly pleasing because it reminded her of the Sussex landscape of their childhood, with 'shady lanes with oak trees in the hedges, a river just under the windows, fields and meadows with paths through them, no stone walls, no miserable looking cabins near it.' Caroline had never been to Ireland – and was to spurn all chances to go – but responded in her own way to what Emily had written. 'What a comfortable little habitation you describe Lord Jocelyn's to be', she wrote, and then went on, moving from the particular to the general as was her wont, 'After all, if there is any difference in situations towards contributing to happiness, that sort of life is the best. But except extreme poverty or extreme greatness – those are undoubtedly the worst – I believe the rest are pretty equal and depend on one's own mind.'

Letter writing gave Caroline the opportunity to look inside herself, record what she found and give it a shape and an order demanded by the etiquette of correspondence that required what was written to be both spontaneous like a conversation and in a 'formed', pleasing style. Writing letters was like writing one's autobiography over many chapters and many years. But receiving letters, too, especially from family members was part of that process, since letters received were the responses to letters written and thus another kind of record of one's life. Through the letters they received, the Lennox sisters assembled archives of their own lives that might be left for their children and posterity or might be simply for their own enjoyment. Emily self-consciously annotated and packaged letters she received and put them aside in a quite deliberate attempt to assemble a record of her life for future generations – perhaps future generations of her own family, perhaps for a wider audience. Her great archive survived intact until the 1830s, when it was selectively burned and edited, probably by one of her grandsons who was dismayed to find in it so complete a record of the life of Emily's favourite son, Lord Edward Fitzgerald, the military commander of the fateful Irish uprising of 1798. Two thousand letters were still left when he had finished, but the politics had almost all gone. That left a marvellous record of Emily's domestic and romantic life, but very few letters after 1794, when Lord Edward's treasonable activities began in earnest, and no letters from the wider circle of politicians Emily knew well,

LEFT
Caroline, painted by Allan Ramsay in 1763–6, with her '*visage de quarante ans*'. Although she self-consciously dressed as an older woman, Caroline was only touching 40 at the time and expected to live to a comfortable old age. In fact she died of cancer at the age of 51.

including her brother the 3rd Duke of Richmond and her nephew Charles James Fox. Emily's archive was taken to South Africa, from where it was bought by a Dublin bookseller and sold on to the National Library in Dublin.

Caroline's papers were similarly doctored, again in the nineteenth century, and probably by the executors and biographers of her son Charles James Fox. This time the opposite principle applied. Fox's executors, and especially their children, had thoughts only for his political legacy. They believed that his domestic activities were unimportant and they were, besides, appalled at his financial and sexual profligacy.

So early on everything in his parents' archive that was not political was thrown out. Finally in 1907 all of Fox's personal papers were put to the flames, a tragic destruction not only of his life and personality, but also his parents'. There was enough left of the Holland House archive, however, for it to become one of the biggest family collections in the British Library after it was deposited by the family in the 1960s.

Louisa and Sarah were also systematic amateur archivists. Louisa's letters constituted for her a personal and private story that she liked to revisit when her sisters were away and the Castletown evenings long. Thus when, in 1767,

ABOVE

Louisa Conolly's bureau in Castletown House. She spent a good deal of time sitting at it, not only writing letters, but looking over the household accounts and making notes on her own expenditure. She kept all the family letters she received bundled up and in drawers, but left instructions that they should be burned at her death.

Sarah begged Louisa to burn a letter that she had sent from Paris, where she was carrying on a dangerous flirtation with the Duc de Lauzun, Louisa replied, 'I can't find it in my heart to burn your letter. It diverts me so much to read it, and now that I have answered it, I shall deposit it in my Safe Drawer. What I call my Safe Drawer is one within a cabinet where I put all my letters tied up in papers, and a written direction for them to be burned unopen'd when I am dead. In the meantime I divert myself with reading them.' Castletown's inheritor Edward Pakenham and Louisa's nephew George Napier were faithful to her wishes. They burned everything after Louisa's

death in 1821 and not a single private letter written to her survives, although her household accounts and other miscellaneous papers were left in Castletown and eventually found their way to the library of Trinity College, Dublin. Sarah's sons similarly destroyed her papers, fearing especially that details of her affairs in the 1760s would leak out and taint their mother's reputation after her death. Sarah's daughter Emily Napier, who had been brought up in Castletown by Louisa, pulled out her aunt's letters to her mother, and Sarah's sons saved a few letters between their parents and letters they themselves had written. The rest were lost. Emily Napier took Louisa's letters to Barton House in Suffolk when she married the nephew of Sarah's first husband Charles Bunbury. They remained there until sold at auction in the 1960s and thereafter became the property of the Irish Georgian Society.

Quiet evenings in town were often spent in the company of family and friends. In Caroline's case that often meant several friends, for Henry Fox was compulsively sociable and liked to have people constantly around him. Caroline was censorious about her husband's *bonhomie*, writing to Emily in 1759, 'Mr Fox with all his good sense does not know people at all, and so my brother often observes, admires people too much for being good company and clever, which after all is nothing valuable unless its attended with as much good nature as he has with it.' She had her own very definite ideas about the necessary qualities of a good acquaintance and worked hard to find enough of them to fill Holland House and satisfy both her stringent requirements and Henry's gregariousness. 'The most entertaining companions in my opinion are people that know a good deal of books and mankind. In short, I think men of learning that have travelled and are communicative are infinitely preferable to people of wit, particularly if they have any imagination with it, a thing much wanting in numbers.' Lawyers like Lord Shelburne (before their acrimonious split in 1763), writers like Horace Walpole and Frances Greville, eccentrics like George Selwyn and Lady Townshend and travellers like Lady Hervey and the great Italophile Clotworthy Upton: these were Caroline's ideal after-dinner guests. They mingled happily at Holland House with men like Topham Beauclerc and George Townshend, whom Henry Fox loved for their wit, and Richard Rigby and John Calcraft, political protégées who were also bonhomous and notorious drinkers.

Dublin, on the other hand, and at the Conollys', could be merely lounging and dull. Louisa complained vigorously in 1782, during the negotiations for the reforms to the Irish constitution that relaxed the penal laws, of 'the

torment of perpetual company, occasioned by the Parliament sitting so late, that all the *Idlers* are in Town, who of course come to us ... sometimes it is ... bearable; at other times intolerable, and I oftener feel more cross about it than I ought to be.'

One dampener on racy town nights was a large family and the number of tiring pregnancies that that implied. Caroline solved the problem of apportioning enough time to her husband, her family and her friends by admitting her children to the adult world as soon as they could walk and by keeping an open political house while she was at Holland House, so that Henry and his cronies were always with her. The Fox children were precocious and prodigious from the start. Charles James Fox attended banquets at Holland House as a toddler and read novels at the age of five. Ste and he were taken to the theatre as soon as they

ABOVE

Tankard and inkstand from the mid-eighteenth century. Besides inkstands, other important paraphernalia of writing were sealing wax and rings with individual seals engraved on them which gave the seal a personal imprint. Letters had no envelopes: some were simply folded and sealed, others folded in an extra sheet of paper and sealed. The recipient paid for the letter by weight on receipt, unless the sender had the use of a frank.

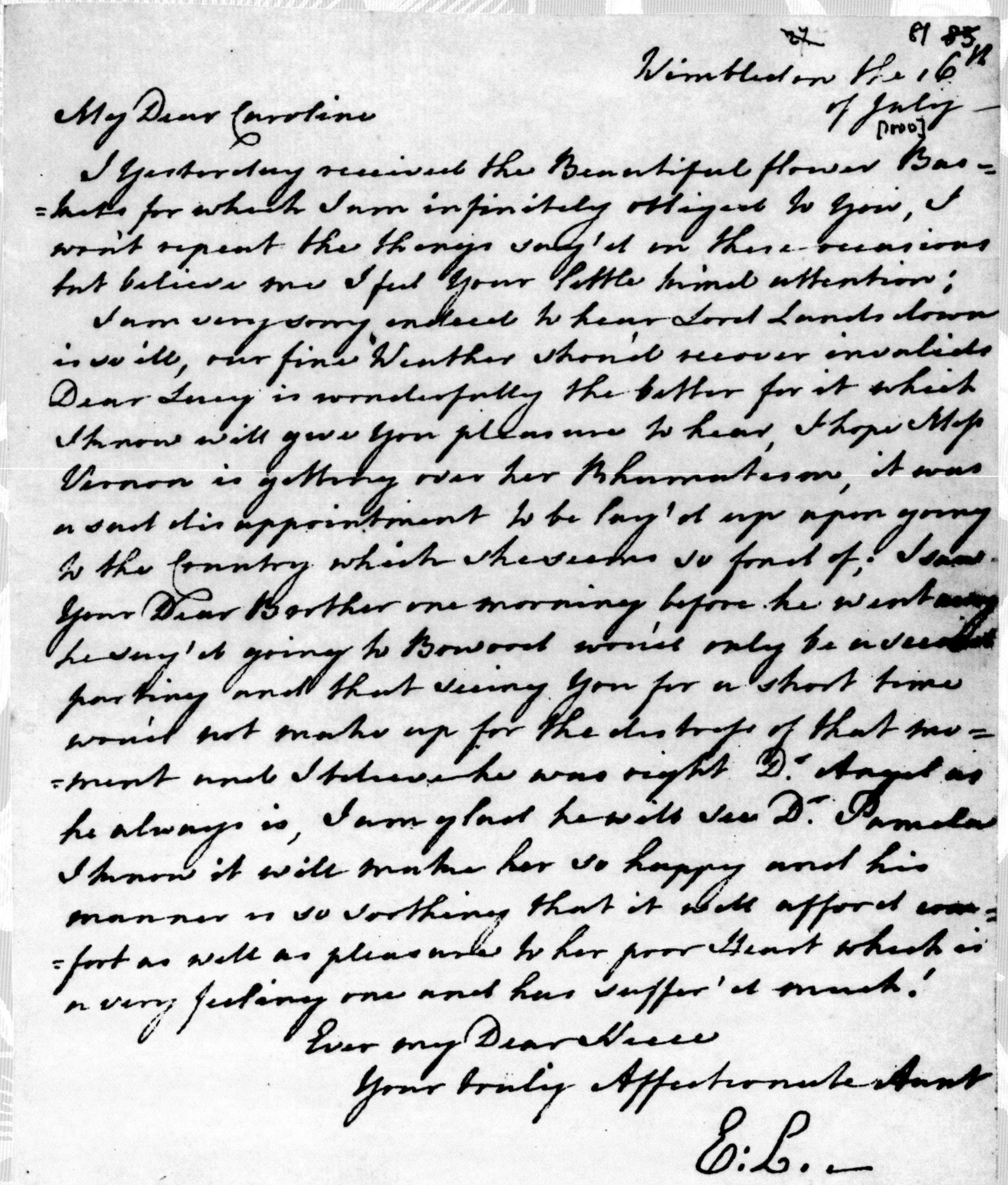

Wimbledon the 16th
of July —
[1790]

My Dear Caroline

I Yesterday received the Beautiful flower Bas=
=kets for which I am infinitely obliged to You, I
won't repeat the things say'd on these occasions
but believe me I feel Your little kind attention;
I am very sorry indeed to hear Lord Lansdown
is so ill, our fine Weather shou'd recover invalids
Dear Lucy is wonderfully the better for it which
I know will give You pleasure to hear, I hope Miss
Vernon is getting over her Rheumatism, it was
a sad disappointment to be lay'd up upon going
to the Country which she seems so fond of; I saw
Your Dear Brother one morning before he went away
he say'd going to Bowood would only be a week
parking and that seeing You for a short time
wou'd not make up for the distress of that mo=
=ment and I believe he was right Dr Angel as
he always is, I am glad he will see Dr Pamela
I know it will make her so happy and his
manner is so soothing that it will afford com=
=fort as well as pleasure to her poor Heart which is
a very feeling one and has suffer'd much.

Ever my Dear Neice
Your truly Affectionate Aunt

E: L: —

could sit through it, infant men about town.

Emily, by contrast, was strongly influenced by the educational theories of Jean Jacques Rousseau, who stressed more strongly than his predecessors like John Locke the childishness and innocence of children. She was happy to allow her children occasional visits to the Smock Alley and Crow Street theatres in Dublin, but unwilling to treat them as adults. The Duke of Leinster, too, drew a firm distinction between the child and the adult worlds; unlike Caroline and Henry, for instance, he never allowed his children's amateur theatricals to be acted in front of friends or political associates, confining their audience to their immediate family and the Carton servants.

Emily and her husband sent their eldest two boys to London at the age of seven or so. They went to Mr Pampellone's academy in Wandsworth with the Fox boys and from there to Eton College. In the holidays they went to Holland House for a taste of metropolitan life. But after the death of her heir and favourite, George, in 1765, Emily refused to be parted from any of her children. She cut herself off from London, staying almost year-round with them in Ireland, living at Carton House and making frequent visits to the school she set up for her large brood at Black Rock by the sea south of Dublin. Her family thought she was buried in the country, as Louisa explained in a

letter from London in January 1773. 'Upon my saying that it was difficult for you to give up the brats, my Brother Richmond says, "She don't suckle them, she don't wean them herself, and she can't cut their teeth for them – why won't she come?" Thinks I, "This is pretty language from a person that knows what treasures they are." But the thing is, they want to see you, and from not knowing the little dears, have no idea of what it would be to you to leave them.' Neither Louisa nor her brother knew, of course, that country life had come to have charms for Emily beyond the pleasures of its own soothing routines.

CHAPTER 3

Country Life

RIGHT
Lady Louisa Conolly in Court dress painted by Allan Ramsay when she arrived in London as a young bride in 1759 aged 15. The portrait was commissioned by Caroline for the Holland House gallery and emphasized Louisa's womanly figure which her sisters regarded as her finest feature.

DESPITE THE FACT THAT her own experiment with living the life of a country lady had ended with her abandonment of both husband and home, Sarah Lennox maintained a romance of country life, of its slower rhythms and the importance of children in its scheme of things. Writing to Emily from Goodwood, where she had been given sanctuary by her brother after she had left first her husband Sir Charles Bunbury and then her lover Lord William Gordon almost a decade earlier, she still, in the depths of loneliness and unhappiness, thought of a country life as the most desirable. 'In most of my imaginary dreams of the happiest state in life, I always represent to myself a husband, wife and children living in a pretty country house, with just neighbours enough to make them enjoy Madame de Sévigny's pleasure of being rid of them; but the chief part of that life being spent just as you spend yours at Aubigny, busy with education, and amused with reading in a family way in the evenings – I must not forget a little planting and improvements, just to keep one out a good deal and make one fancy one has got a great deal of business which enlivens one.'

Sarah wrote this letter to Emily in 1778. Caroline and Lord Holland had been dead four years, dying within a month of each other in 1774. Lord Holland died of a stroke compounded by old age and boredom; Caroline from cancer. Their son Ste, 2nd Lord Holland died soon after 1775, leaving the title to his infant son Henry. Sarah had been living on the Goodwood estate for nine lonely years, fighting low spirits and getting into trouble with her brothers for meddling in their family affairs. Emily was no longer at

Emily's children in the grounds of Carton House. Sometimes she almost despaired about being continually pregnant, but declared stoically, 'I have resolved not to grumble. After all, are not my pretty babes a blessing?'

Carton. When the Duke of Leinster died in 1773, she shocked her family and scandalized Dublin society by marrying her children's tutor, William Ogilvie. Bequeathed Carton House for life unless she married again, Emily cannily made it over to her son William, 2nd Duke of Leinster, in exchange for a large sum of money, while her marriage was still a secret. Black Rock, her children's school house, remained to her, but instead of going to live there she had left it in the care of Louisa Conolly and departed for France and a new life. William Ogilvie and her large brood – Charlotte, Sophia, Edward,

Robert, Gerald, Fanny, Lucy, Louisa and George Fitzgerald – were with her. The Carton money, her own jointure of £4,000 a year and the late Duke's generous allowances for his children meant that they could live extremely comfortably in France, where goods were cheap, and still spend a good deal on renovating Black Rock to suit Emily's expensive tastes. By the time Sarah wrote, the family was settled at the Duke of Richmond's château at Aubigny, and Emily had added her last two children, Cecilia and Mimi Ogilvie to the nest.

Only Louisa's life had been unruffled by the

passing years. In 1778 she was 35. Still childless, still with Tom Conolly and still at her beloved Castletown, which she now rarely left, she had grown without regret into middle age, and her childlessness had reinforced her role of comforter and confidante to the rest of the

family. Now she had the residue of Emily's Irish life to look after as well as the constant anxiety of Sarah's future.

Louisa had never wavered in her devotion to country life. As time went on this love was reinforced by her dislike of cities, London and

BELOW
Emily and Lord Kildare painted by Arthur Devis in the 1750s; a studio painting with an imaginary Carton in the background.

BELOW
Carton House,
County Kildare.
Now the front, this was
the back of the house in
Emily's time.

Dublin in particular. Building and decorating at Castletown, walking with her dogs, spending days or sometimes weeks with Emily and the Fitzgerald children at Carton when Tom Conolly was occupied with his hunters or racing and the

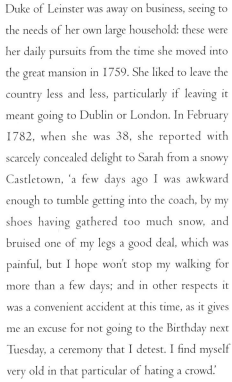

Duke of Leinster was away on business, seeing to the needs of her own large household: these were her daily pursuits from the time she moved into the great mansion in 1759. She liked to leave the country less and less, particularly if leaving it meant going to Dublin or London. In February 1782, when she was 38, she reported with scarcely concealed delight to Sarah from a snowy Castletown, 'a few days ago I was awkward enough to tumble getting into the coach, by my shoes having gathered too much snow, and bruised one of my legs a good deal, which was painful, but I hope won't stop my walking for more than a few days; and in other respects it was a convenient accident at this time, as it gives me an excuse for not going to the Birthday next Tuesday, a ceremony that I detest. I find myself very old in that particular of hating a crowd.'

Country houses like Castletown and Carton were neither the oases of calm that their owners sometimes liked to suggest, nor the quiet sepulchral museums of two hundred years later. They buzzed with life and were run to the sound of bells. If ladies of the house had boudoirs and closets of their own, it was partly because they needed spaces that really were private and tranquil. House maids ran up and down the backstairs with washing and mending, coal and water; ladies maids took deliveries of millinery and clothes upstairs for their mistresses to try on and discuss; men servants loitered in the butlers'

pantry or the still-room; butlers came with drinks; there were stable-hands, coachmen, carpenters and the steward, cooks and blacksmiths and gardeners all making a busy show of going about their work.

Besides its owners, then, a country house was home to scores of people. The top floors of houses like Carton and Castletown were divided into dozens of small rooms with sash-windows that peaked through the roof leads and were concealed behind the balustrade. Up to thirty young women might sleep there in the gods: nursery maids, house maids, visiting servants. At Carton a small spiral staircase ran without interruption from the top floor into the Duke of

Leinster's own suite of rooms two floors below, a manifestation of his visiting rights and his droit de seigneur.

Below the maids at Carton lived the children and their own servants; below them again the Duke and Duchess and their guests. Footmen, cooks and kitchen hands lived above the kitchen and the offices in the wings that ran off the main house; coachmen, gardeners and other outside servants lived in the stable yard and above the stables themselves. Married couples lived elsewhere on the estate or in neighbouring villages; but night and day country houses were busy places, full from top to bottom.

A rough division of responsibility beween

ABOVE

The shell cottage, Carton, with Sarah – Jodhi May – Emily – Geraldine Somerville – and their little sister Cecelia – played by Charlotte Moynihan – picking out shells for designs. Emily called such projects 'the greatest amusement in the world', but that was before she met William Ogilvie and embarked on a life of obsessive passion.

ABOVE

Kildare – Ben Daniels – and Emily – Geraldine Somerville – and their children by the lake at Carton. A herd of cows grazed in the park. 'I wish you could see the cows in the park', Emily wrote to Kildare when he was away in London in the 1750s, 'they look so pretty and eat such fine mouthfuls of grass and seem to enjoy it so.'

master and mistress was made in running the house and the estate. The mistress was, according to an unwritten rule, responsible for the female staff and all that they did. In the chain of command the housekeeper answered directly to the mistress of the house and was responsible for all the maids and their duties: the cleaning and laundry, the mending and making of fires, the airing and ironing and tidying up. The steward, who was the senior household servant, looked after the estate, collected the rents and was responsible for provisioning from the home farm. He answered to the master of the house, and ran a team of gardeners, handymen, shepherds and carters, besides carrying ultimate responsibility for what went on on the whole estate. Alongside both steward and housekeeper worked the butler who was in charge of bought-in provisions like the groceries and the wine cellar, and who supervised the footmen and the

pantry boys, and the clerk of the kitchen who ran the forbidding operation of cooking for the entire 'family' as the inhabitants of the house were called.

At Castletown Louisa quickly grew to enjoy her role as mistress of the household. While Tom Conolly amused himself with wheels and carriages, hunters and steeplechasers, she checked the household accounts and fussed over the dairy and the hothouses. Although over the years the Conollys' huge programme of building guaranteed a certain level of debt, Castletown was an extremely well-run household with a loyal core of staff.

Emily's style at Carton was rather different. She had no interest in household management; if she noticed something amiss her solution was to spare no expense in putting it right. Henry Fox loved to tease Emily about her extravagance, and said there was no point in berating her for

BELOW
The 2nd Duke and Duchess of Leinster walking by his father's lake at Carton, painted by Thomas Roberts in the late 1770s. The lake was designed almost 20 years earlier and the banks were by this time well covered with trees and shrubs.

RIGHT

Skating at Castletown, painted by Robert Healy. The Duke of Leinster cuts an elegant figure in the centre with Louisa's beloved dog Hibou behind him. The other two figures are surely his heir William and William's tutor Bolle. William and Bolle were abroad in the winter of 1768, which casts doubt on the usual dating of the picture to that year. In addition, Louisa's dog Hibou disappeared in the summer of 1768, so this painting could not have been done that winter unless from memory or by copying earlier pictures.

Emily being driven around the Carton Park by her hump-backed coachman, painted by William Ashford in the 1760s; perhaps on one of the 'jumbling' rides she recommended for the later stages of pregnancy.

being an atrocious housekeeper: as Caroline teasingly reported to her in 1759, 'Mr Fox is extremely concern'd to hear of any distress occasion'd by your indolence and carelessness, he says, being well assured that your domestic activity will never be worth to the Earl of Kildare above three crowns per annum.' Carton House, everyone suspected, ran better when Emily took no interest in it; a bustle of activity

only translated into a mountain of bills. In November 1762, for instance, Emily examined all the linen at Carton, noting proudly, 'I really think I have made myself a tolerable mistress of this business', and cheerfully reporting to her absent husband, 'I have been employed these three mornings, my dearest Lord Kildare, in laying out most immense sums for you: coarse sheets without end, upper servants' sheets, small sheets for the children's beds, fine holland sheets for the middle floor at Carton and for our own use, table-cloths for the steward's table … plate cloths, waiting napkins, rubbers, in short all sorts of necessaries to the amount I believe of £150.'

While Louisa's household was Irish from top to bottom, with the exception, perhaps, of a French or English maid for herself, Emily and Kildare tended to import servants with special skills. They had a French confectioner whose job it was to make the multi-storeyed and multi-coloured puddings for grand dinners as well as sweetmeats for Emily's everyday consumption.

They had an English housekeeper, and as the children grew up they had French – or, if possible, French-speaking Swiss Protestant – servants to talk French and 'be about' them, as Emily put it. These servants had two functions: to improve the children's French, and to make sure that they picked up neither too strong a brogue nor too strong a dose of Catholicism or 'superstition', as Louisa reminded Emily in 1776. 'The poor dear Irish', she wrote, in the middle of a passage extolling the virtues of having French servants, 'partial as I am in general to them, I know are abominable upon

LEFT

The Carton carriage wash, showing the car wash was invented long before the car. Carriages were driven between the two semicircles and washed by the coachmen standing on the walls. Thus elevated the men could wash the carriage roofs, which was important because carriages were often seen from above by hosts and hostesses standing on the flights of steps that led up to the grandest front doors.

ABOVE

The back of Carton House. This was the front in Emily's day. RIGHT Emily, pregnant with the future Lord Edward Fitzgerald, and perhaps seated because of this, painted by Allan Ramsay in 1765. 'I like it of all things and think it very like', Caroline wrote when her version of the painting arrived at Holland House in 1766.

these occasions, and are very apt to fill the children's heads with nonsense.'

It followed that one of the least agreeable tasks that attended London visits was that of finding servants willing to come to Ireland, and negotiating terms with them. In 1759 Emily had to find a gardener to supervise the making of their new park and gardens at Carton. Henry Fox, whose father had founded the Royal Military Hospital and Physic Garden at Chelsea when he was Paymaster of the Forces, used his contacts to come up with a young man who had been trained there. 'He has never lived with any family ... was bred up in the physic garden, and has of late undertaken pieces of work by contract and understands layout.' Despite this mixed report, Emily was for hiring him straight away and concluding her task. 'Upon the whole I am for agreeing with him, as everybody allows

'tis such a difficulty to get them to go to Ireland; none but those who are undone and can't live here will [go].'

It was important to hire suitable senior servants because in Ireland they frequently dined with the family, and the master and mistress of the household were required to spend a good deal of time with them. Often, indeed, the contract between master and servant became an emotionally charged one in which, although boundaries of class always remained, shared experience and interests led to complicated but real friendships. Emily's housekeeper in the late 1760s, a well-educated woman called Mrs Lynch, and her maid Rowley, both followed her to France when she left Ireland in 1774. Mrs Lynch became much more than housekeeper; she was, as Emily put it, 'a second mother' to the youngest Fitzgeralds and the Ogilvie children.

The Foxes' steward and housekeeper were, conveniently, a married couple, Mr and Mrs Fannen, with whom they were on excellent terms. Yet despite this closeness, neither Emily nor Caroline wrote anything in their letters about their relative social or economic positions. Caroline had a bleak, essentially pessimistic vision of the world. She was fearful of the power of the 'mob', as she called it, and dismissive of claims popular leaders like John Wilkes made for an extension of political power to greater numbers of people. Emily, in contrast, perhaps because of her immersion in the opposition politics of the Duke of Leinster, became

interested in rights and reform of government. But nowhere did she advocate any redistribution of wealth or shift in the social hierarchy, believing, for a start, that she herself was provided with wholly inadequate funds.

It was left to Louisa, rich and without children to provide for, to look around her at Castletown and in the villages beyond its park, and to turn her ethic of duty into a moral code which necessarily had some political implications. She had always endeavoured to live according to simple moral and religious principles. In September 1772, when she was 29, she wrote to Sarah, 'doing and thinking right

LEFT
The salon at Carton House. The ceiling, by the Lafranchini brothers, was put up in 1739 before Kildare inherited the house, but the organ was installed in the mid-nineteenth century. ABOVE The India paper room at Carton, created by Emily and Louisa in 1760. It was Emily's boudoir, where she lived all day in the winter, and it looked out into the garden.

is our business from our cradle to the day of our death. That we don't do it is but too certain, but our endeavours ought to be constant.' By then, almost a decade of peace had taken some of the steam out of the Irish economy, and she had begun to feel the burden of responsibility not only for her immediate household but also for the poor whom she saw all around her. She concluded, unusually for someone in her position, that the disparity of wealth between rich and poor was simply too wide. 'Perhaps I am wrong in my ideas of society,' she told Sarah. 'But my notion is, that the division is very unfair between rich and poor. A distinction I know is

necessary for the sake of subordination, but less difference with respect to riches, and a rigid exactness with respect to the established laws I should think would equally keep people in order, and certainly they would be more comfortable. I speak with respect to this country, where really the greater number (without exaggeration) have a bare subsistence, and their wretched way of subsisting hardly deserves the name of subsistence. The laws are seldom put in force, and their poverty is such a temptation to be dishonest, that the greater part are so, but the cause seems plain, and if removed, one might hope in time to make them honest and happy.'

LEFT
The view south from Castletown House to the Dublin mountains.
ABOVE The Green Drawing Room at Castletown, one of a series of rooms on the *piano nobile* that were architecturally finished if not decorated or fully furnished when Louisa moved in.

As time went on, Louisa's sense of responsibility towards the poor increased, although her compassion was always more religious than political in origin and direction. From her early thirties she was actively involved in charitable work in Dublin and around her estate. After Tom Conolly's death in 1803, her impulses found full expression. She closed down much of the house, transformed Tom's stable block into an ecumenical school for local girls and boys, and employed as many men as she could on building schemes in the park. Released from the need to be a great lady, she became a philanthropist instead. But Louisa had always wanted to be good and to do good; she started with her family, widened her circle to include her household after her marriage, and ended her life as a general and much-loved benefactor to

LEFT
The first-floor passageway at Castletown, part of the scheme of the great entrance hall.
BELOW The Red Drawing Room, finished and decorated by Louisa as one of her first tasks on arrival.

Looking up through the base of one of the three Venetian chandeliers in the Castletown long gallery. Louisa was immensely proud of her specially selected chandeliers in blue, pink and clear crystal glass. Their cheerful informality fits her decorative scheme much better than the more common monumental Waterford crystal chandeliers that would otherwise have hung there.

the poor in her neighbourhood. When she died, scores of poor people were allowed to see her body as it lay in state, and hundreds lined the long main street of Celbridge as her coffin passed down it.

In the early years, though, Louisa, like her sisters, enjoyed improvements more for the pleasure they gave those who planned them than for the employment they gave those who carried them out. Emily, in particular, showed nothing but impatience with her painters, decorators and gardeners, convinced of their tardiness, inefficiency and incompetence. Caroline, who

with Henry was engaged in the 1760s in transforming the modest country estate of Kingsgate on the North Foreland in Kent into a spectacular jumble of follies, ruins, gardens and a villa, simply never mentioned the tiresome process of building itself, preferring instead to stress her husband's 'amusement' in the works and the benefits to his health of the good air and his fantastic projects.

Throughout the 1750s and '60s Carton and its park were huge building sites, where up to three hundred workmen might be employed at one time. Inside the house, Emily redecorated

LEFT

Louisa's meticulously planned and miraculously preserved print room at Castletown, slowly created in the 1760s and 1770s. A print of Reynolds's monumental sublime portrait of Sarah, *Lady Sarah Bunbury Sacrificing to the Graces*, hangs in the centre of the left-hand wall, while Reynolds's *Garrick between Comedy and Tragedy* is in the middle of the group above the fireplace.

RIGHT

A bas-relief profile of Emily created by the Lafranchini brothers at the top of the staircase in the main hall at Castletown in the early 1760s. Emily was a second mother to Louisa, and although she lived only a few miles away, Louisa filled Castletown with mementoes of her and of her other siblings, particularly Sarah. 'I am wild about pictures of you and my sister Kildare', she admitted to Sarah, adding, 'I don't think I shall ever be satisfied without dozens of them.'

the series of state rooms at the front on the ground floor, created an 'India paper room' for herself on the garden side, made a print room with her sisters and daughters and bought furniture, pictures and books for the library. Outside, under the testy supervision of the Duke of Leinster, the park was redesigned and sculpted into fashionable informality with an artificial lake surrounded by woodland, a new Palladian bridge across the water and a sinewy driveway from the Dublin road up to the house. The park was landscaped with clumps of beeches, oaks and acacias, while showy cedars were planted around the house in ones and twos.

Emily constructed a shell cottage by the lake side and established a formal garden with 'shady walks' and rose bushes.

Despite the fact that this whole scheme seriously compromised the family finances, Emily and her sisters persisted in describing their passion for improvements as an 'amusement'. Caroline went further, calling it 'rational' and writing to Emily in 1768, when the Kingsgate improvements were in full swing and Emily, having finished off Carton, was turning her attentions to her seaside villa at Black Rock, 'I agree with you that a taste for trifling amusements is a great happiness. Perhaps I go

ABOVE

The Brown Study, Castletown. Panelled in oak, this room was one of the few completed before Louisa moved in, when the house was occupied by Tom Conolly's aunt, who lived in just a few rooms and left most of the great edifice empty and unfinished.

139

LEFT
A bedroom at Castletown. Louisa's bedroom reportedly had purple hangings and curtains tied back with bowed ribbons.
RIGHT Louisa's boudoir, created around 1770 and showing the same taste for informality and a kind of monumental homeliness as is evident in the long gallery.

FAR LEFT AND LEFT
Two views of Castletown's great hallway, paved in a chequerboard of marble and stuccoed to the full height of its double cube. To complement the portrait of Emily in one plaster roundel was a portrait of her husband Kildare in another. The grandeur of the total effect made it immediately clear to visitors that they were entering the house of Ireland's richest man.

further; I think when one is young nothing is so rational, nothing else is worthwhile. Apropos to that you have no idea what a beautiful blue and white paper I have just put up in the salon here; its really exceedingly pretty and quite new.' Not content with overseeing the building works, they began to design their own alterations too. Architectural design was thought of as a male preserve. By the eighteenth century it was regarded as acceptable, even fashionable, for a gentleman to turn his hand to building design: Lord Burlington, for instance, or, on a much smaller scale, Lord Kildare with his Palladian bridge at Carton. The Lennox women,

however, clearly also saw design as a legitimate occupation. Louisa created the eclectically informal Castletown long gallery and print room and had a series of outdoor buildings constructed according to her own plans. In 1761, barely eighteen months after moving into Castletown, Louisa had already begun her programme of improvements, as she explained to Sarah: 'I have a lodge abuilding, a little dear, tidy one of my own drawing, which is a prodigious entertainment to me. I also have a dairy abuilding, which I am very fond of. Its so pleasant I think to have some work going on that one looks over oneself.'

Two years later Louisa had finished Castletown's marble and stucco entrance hall and begun on the grand rooms of the rest of the *piano nobile*. Outside she was building a cottage in the woods that Emily so envied, where she would sit and write in the summer mornings, watching tame foxes that she had released from domestication play among the trees in front of her open door. By 1768, the house and grounds were in so good a state that the Conollys began adding bits to their park. 'This is the loveliest day that ever was,' Louisa wrote to Sarah in March 1768, 'so pray take it as a compliment my staying in the house to write to you. There are also gilders in the house,

just come to new gild the frames of our pictures in the dining room. All this finishing work is mighty entertaining. I am as busy as a bee ... We have also got a little addition of ground by the river side. 'Tis a very little bit, but ... having a new thing to do is mighty pleasant.' Ten years later these improvements to the park were still not finished. 'Nobody can be busier than I by the riverside,' she told Sarah in the spring of 1779. 'The pond is turned into a river and three cascades made in a cut, that is carried down to the river, which I also think are very pretty. You cannot conceive how much I divert myself here.'

In some of this work, especially in the 1770s, Louisa had help with planning from Sarah, who

RIGHT

Sarah's first husband Sir Charles Bunbury, painted by Joshua Reynolds for the Holland House gallery shortly after their marriage of 1762. When offered this portrait by the 3rd Lord Holland, Bunbury's nephew and heir declined it, saying that he did not wish to be reminded of his uncle. Bunbury was, however, scrupulously fair to Sarah when their marriage collapsed, whatever his private shortcomings.

was reckoned the best artist in the family, and whose son William was a competent enough painter to consider making it a full-time occupation when he was put on half-pay by the army after the end of the Napoleonic Wars. Sarah, having chosen the poorest husband, had the least scope for improvements after her marriage. When she was in exile on her brother's estate after her disgrace, she planned and just had time to move into a new house that he built for her at Moldcomb. But she did not have a house that she could tinker with until the 1780s, when she and her husband George Napier built a house in Celbridge. It was virtually a present from the Conollys, but for the first time Sarah was able to indulge in the sort of dreams and plans that her sisters had been enjoying for decades. Her house was plain and cramped in comparison to theirs; three storeys high, two rooms deep and surrounded by a small garden and orchard. None the less, when it was nearly finished she wrote happily to Susan O'Brien, 'At present I am in full enjoyment of the diversions of fancy and scheming, for my sister and I go there almost every day, sit in the different rooms, which only want papering, and settle how charming each will be: then we admire the orchard in full bloom upon the grass we have lately sown, the turn of a new walk, the look of a clump that is, or is to be.' These delightful activities could be dangerous. In 1782 an over-

eager Emily, just returned to Ireland and Black Rock, fell down a light well while exploring the alterations there. 'She assures me that she is quite well', Louisa told Sarah, but went on anxiously, 'I cannot get it out of my head but that she must have broke a rib, but she says she is sure it is only bruised blood. ... She has had a miraculous escape. Think of her falling down

BELOW
One of the niches in the Castletown Long Gallery, with decorations painted by a Mr Reily. Eight busts of classical worthies were ranged round the room, and classical scenes were painted on the walls.

A silhouette of Sarah in her widowhood by John Miers. Despite her devastation at Napier's death in 1804, Sarah enjoyed her old age and her position as a famous mother of famous sons. RIGHT Sarah's plans of her houses at Moldcomb on the Goodwood estate and in the village of Celbridge by Castletown House.

one of those little places that are made to give light to the rooms below, a place seven feet deep and walled round. How she escaped broken bones, God knows.'

Undeterred by this sort of risk, and not content with transforming their own houses, the Lennox sisters turned their hands to others'. 'Lady Barrymore is going to build a house', Louisa wrote to Emily in 1776, 'I hope by a plan that I am drawing for her, which I think will be just what she wants.' The major work

undertaken in the 1770s, however, was the transformation of Emily's Black Rock villa from a seaside school into a country house. In this scheme Sarah and Louisa both took part, Sarah supplying letters full of plans and ideas, Louisa carrying out the more practical work of organizing carpenters, paying builders and advising and liaising between all the parties.

When the Duke of Leinster bought the house at Black Rock in 1765, it was nothing more than a seaside villa for a Dublin gentleman, with a few fields and access to the sea across the Bray road. The house expanded with the school Emily and the Duke established there. Two new wings, incorporating a stable and a dairy, were added, and a kitchen garden established where the children grew vegetables according to Rousseau's prescriptions.

Black Rock soon became a place of refuge for Emily, ostensibly a healthy alternative to the gloom of Leinster House and the bad air of the city. Soon after the end of Emily's confinement following the birth of Augustus in 1767, Louisa told Sarah that although Emily, 'has no particular complaint, her spirits are not very good; but I attribute it to her not having been out in the air, for the weather has been so bad since her month was up that she has not yet ventured out. … I am in hopes that she will go and spend a few days at the Black Rock, which I am sure will be of vast service to her.' Emily's sisters attributed

Ellbridge House.

a Hall & great staircase, back stairs besides
b little book room
c Drawing room, a little odd with 2 corner chimneys, but very comfortable
d. Passage room
d. Closet
e Passage & Stairs to the Offices ⎫ low building
f. Bed & Dressing room

To the South East is a pleasant terrace, with vaulted cellars under it.

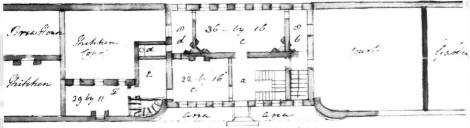

Aspect — North East

Molscomb House.

a Hall & Staircase   i Colonade
b Pantry   h covered passage & blue tiles
c Dining room   l Coal Hole
d Drawing room   m Laundry with a chimney
e Housekeepers room   n Kitchen (no womens
f Colonade   & servants)
g Green House
h Dairy, with a best room over it

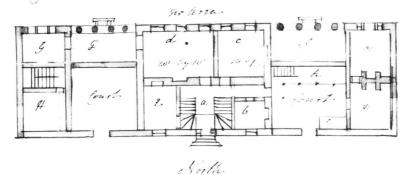

North

10 20 30 40 50   100   150

FAR LEFT
The main staircase at Castletown with its straight brass railing. LEFT Louisa Conolly, a mature woman in an unpretentious lace cap in the 1770s: the conscience and good angel of the family.

her good spirits at Black Rock to the presence of her children and the healthy sea breezes; a few days later Louisa was able to report to Sarah, 'My sister … is quite recovered by going into the country air. You may easily guess what a pleasant thing it is to spend a little time with all the dear children in a sweet pretty little neat house which my sister is making more comfortable every day, nothing fine on account of the brats.'

Soon Emily was spending so much time at Black Rock, especially in the summer, that Louisa decided to buy a house there too. It was, she told Sarah, 'a neat, tidy little place', and, 'there is only a little hedge between our field and my sister's. We have made a gate already, and 'tis so near, that 'tis like being in the same house. The children are continually running in and out, and if the people won't plague me with visiting, I shall be very comfortable here.' Even such close proximity, however, did not alert Louisa to what was really going on over the hedge. She remained in ignorance of the affair between Emily and Ogilvie until after the death of the Duke of Leinster in 1773.

When Emily left for France, she gave Black Rock a grand new Italianate name, Frescati, and put Louisa in charge of the alterations there. But this could be no Carton-style extravaganza. Mr Ogilvie was careful with money and Dublin tradesmen would not give unlimited credit to an absent widowed duchess married to a schoolmaster. One thing did remain the same, though: Emily allowed others to do the work for her. Louisa and Sarah spent days dreaming up plans, modifying drawings, talking to builders and writing long progress reports to their sister. Some of the work was definitely economical. 'I think that if you get a quite plain white marble French chimney made in France or Italy, it would cost very little', Sarah wrote in 1775, and suggested a little do-it-yourself touch to make it look luxurious: 'I think you might get an ormolu oak-leaf branch either in France, or at

Birmingham, and have it appliqué upon the flat part of the chimney, which would be odd, and I think pretty and suit your room.'

Some luxuries, though, her sisters insisted Emily could not do without. En-suite bedrooms and bathrooms had just become fashionable and Louisa decided were Emily's due, as she explained in a letter of 1776. 'Your bedchamber … is without exception the very prettiest and pleasantest bedchamber that ever was. I only wish you would make your little closet next to it into a warm bath and water-closet, and then 'twould be the most complete apartment I know of.' During the years of Emily's absence the house grew, though its origins as a seaside villa were never completely obscured. By the time the family returned in 1781, Frescati had a suite of comfortable rooms on the ground floor, which included a showy round room, a grand drawing-room and a book room overlooking the garden, kitchen, offices, stables and a total of 65 fireplaces.

It took Louisa Conolly a couple of years to get used to life at Castletown after her marriage to Tom. In contrast to the Duke of Leinster, who always insisted on grandeur and style, Tom Conolly lived an informal, squirish life, on free and easy terms with his jockeys and grooms, playing cricket and running races with his guests and happiest of all with his horses at the

LEFT

An inlaid, painted cabinet from Castletown with laquered and inlaid doors. Louisa was very fond of inlay and Caroline offered to send her a fine inlaid piece from Paris during her trip of 1763–4; on the whole her offers were declined, however, because her sisters did not share her taste.

Curragh. Racing, especially, was a new and tedious pastime for Louisa. 'I was at the Curragh all last week and was very much tired of it', she admitted to Sarah eighteen months after her wedding. 'It was miserable weather and no talk of anything but horses, hounds, bets and gambling.' As time went on she learned to leave Conolly and the horses together and to retreat to Carton when the races came round. While Louisa usually went to Carton, which for her was simply

going home, Emily could occasionally be persuaded to visit Castletown. In the autumn of 1762 she spent several weeks there recovering from a difficult labour. She warmed to its informal ways, writing to her husband, 'We are mighty quiet and comfortable, live all day long in one room, muddle and dress in the morning for all day – in short, just the lazy kind of life which you know when once I get into I love mightily, and it is much better for you than if I was losing

RIGHT

Louisa walking with her gamekeeper and a hunting dog in a wintry park, painted by Healy in 1768. While most paintings that included servants had them looking up at their masters or standing to one side of them, servants in this series by Healy occupy prominent positions in the compositions, perhaps because of their importance in the Castletown scheme of things, perhaps because what Tom and Louisa wanted was not so much a series of portraits of themselves as a series of vignettes of their life in the country.

my money at loo in town.' Fifty guineas that she had earmarked for gambling losses remained 'untouched' she reported proudly, and she had even been walking in the woodland, which allowed her to point out the need for such an amenity at Carton. 'That wood is worth a million to people who live here in winter, besides the beauty of it in summer, for to have so charming a walk or ride where no wind comes nor wet underfoot is delightful. Its a pity we poor invalids have not such a one; I hope that is not coveting one's neighbour's goods.'

Although one of the main *raisons d'être* of the country house was the country, Emily rarely indulged in any country pursuits. By temperament she was a townswoman, and indeed lived the last thirty years of her life in London. She did not ride and hardly ever walked. She did sit in her gardens, at Carton, at Aubigny and finally in her small country retreat at Wimbledon to the south west of London. She sometimes walked around the Carton lake with Lord Kildare if the path was sufficiently well gravelled. Most of the time, though, she stayed indoors and for airings drove out in her one-horse chaise. Caroline was equally uninterested in vigorous exercise and in all her long correspondence never mentioned herself hunting, riding, walking or enjoying the outdoors beyond the confines of her parks and gardens. Her letters from Kingsgate in Kent concentrated on the passive benefits of country life; pure air, early and regular hours and no casual visitors to distract her husband.

Sarah and, especially Louisa, were much more enthusiastic country dwellers, perhaps because they had spent most of their childhoods at Carton, without the long London breaks that the 2nd Duke of Richmond's court life necessitated for Caroline and Emily. Sarah threw herself into country life in Suffolk after her marriage in 1762. She had her own hunter, started a garden and surrounded herself with animals that were both surrogate children and, in the frequent absences of her husband, day-to-day companions. Less than four months after her wedding she had acquired a creature whose mechanical responses were uncannily like those of Charles Bunbury himself. 'I have got such a parrot as never was heard of', she told Emily. 'It never bites nor screams. It says every morning, "Polly, Avez-vous dejourné? oui, oui, oui, oui! Et de quoi? De la rotie." It says Dragon pour boire, Pretty Polly say, and a song like an old Frenchman; and besides has all the conversation of other parrots. Add to this that it has a yellow head, green body spotted with yellow, and scarlet tops to its wings. In short I adore it.'

By 1766 Sarah was using her jokey letters to her friend Susan O'Brien to send scarcely disguised signals about the state of her marriage. Her animals, she said, had first place in Suffolk,

LEFT

The stables at
Castletown –
luxury homes for Tom's
beloved beasts. After
Tom's death Louisa
used the stable block
for a school for local
children, but it
eventually reverted to
its original use.

and, she hinted, in her heart. 'My creatures are the people of first consequence here', she told Susan in February 1766. 'I have got an Angola cat that is so beautiful that she is the admiration of all the country; I am distractedly fond of her, and she is never from me a moment, having one great perfection that endears her to me, and that is, she puts me in mind of you in her looks from morning till night, and has the slyest, prettiest look that I ever saw in anybody but you or her.'

Animals faded out of Sarah's letters when adultery leached in as their hidden subject. But in the years after her flight from Barton House with Lord William Gordon in 1769, the long period of ostracism and isolation in Sussex, when she and her illegitimate daughter Louisa often spent weeks alone, her 'creatures' were once again her constant companions and a subject for her letters. The demise of her dog Ranger in 1779 was a footnote to her own desolation, as she explained to Emily. 'I have not mended my spirits by the loss of my poor dog Ranger, who died after three days illness, between Louisa and I, just as we were watching him. ...[I] did not bear his death with heroism, I confess.'

There were dogs everywhere at Castletown too. Mr Conolly kept a pack of hounds from the late 1760s onwards, but before that there were farm dogs, hunting dogs and Tom and Louisa's own pets, the latter lolling round the house and 'perfuming the air not a little' as she put it. In the

Louisa, a groom, Hibou and a horse. Louisa is painted here by Healy ready to mount, her riding crop in her hand, but in fact riding was not her favourite activity. She much preferred a trudge round the park, either on her own or with a sister or friend for company, and on fine days would find activity there for a whole day outdoors.

1760s Louisa went everywhere with her little dog Hibou and was painted with him strolling through the park in her simple walking habit. Writing to Sarah, Louisa routinely sent messages from the menagerie. 'Hibou desires his duty', she reported in May 1768. 'Just now he saw me putting on my hat, which rejoiced him, as he knows 'tis time to go out. He is very impatient, so God bless you … my dearest Sal, Ever Yrs LAC.' Soon afterwards, Hibou went missing and Louisa confided sadly, 'I have never found poor Hibou'. Offers of dogs poured in and a surrogate, Joke, was put on the Dublin boat and the cart to Castletown, a present from the 3rd Duke of Richmond.

With one or more dogs bounding about her, and accompanied by guests or relatives if she could persuade them to get up, Louisa took a walk immediately before or after breakfast whenever she could. 'Ciss is waiting for me to go a-walking with her', she told Sarah in a letter from Carton in the 1760s. ''Tis not much after seven, and I have wrote this letter to you this morning, so you see how early we are.' At Castletown she often walked about alone. 'You know the pleasant way one dawdles away one's time in the country,' she confided to Sarah one January day in the early 1770s, saying, 'By the by, if the snow should not be gone by the time you receive this letter, I must tell you of a pretty diversion that I have found out, that you may

LEFT

Tom Conolly at full gallop on one of his racehorses. Before the way in which horses galloped was photographed and understood, painters usually depicted them in this way, legs outstretched like rocking horses.

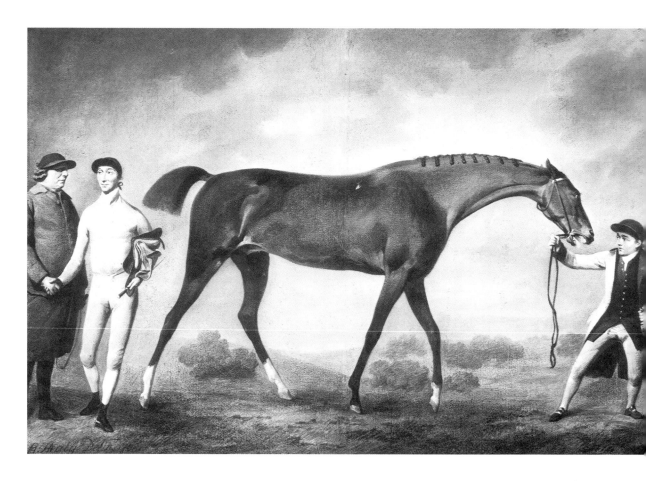

ABOVE

A different, but no less important beast, with three white feet instead of four black ones. Conolly is seen here shaking hands with his trainer, probably before an important race or challenge, while his horse proves his metal by looking menacingly at the stable hand.

have the same at Goodwood among the evergreens; and that is touching the snow on the branches gently with a little stick, which makes them all get up again like the machinery in a Harlequin farce. I was such a little miss as to divert myself a whole morning doing this, but its good for the plants, as the weight of snow lying on them is apt to break them.'

Although Sarah, Caroline and especially Louisa, liked to stress how separate the country was from the town, some of the ebb and flow of people in the country was caused by the duties of town life. The country filled up when the town emptied: when Parliament went into recess, when

the Season ended and when the monarch himself left town. Summer, early autumn and Christmas were the busiest periods in country houses, and letters sent at those times could give the illusion that country life was a continuous house party. In September 1771, Louisa reported to Sarah that she and Emily had just left the seaside for Carton House. 'The next day being fine we went to the Cottage in the morning, dined there, and spent the whole day sauntering about the nursery and kissing Lucy, who is just the right mumbling age ... I came home and found Mr Conolly returned from the Curragh. Our weather is most delightful which he makes use of to go out shooting, and I shall tomorrow be busy the whole day planting.'

At Christmastime both Carton and Castletown saw a month of house parties and festivities. Emily and Louisa were both loath to accept invitations – Emily because she refused either to leave or to take her children, Louisa because she disliked leaving her home – so friends and acquaintances came to them. In 1776, Louisa proudly reported to Emily the successful inauguration of her newly decorated long gallery, explaining, '18 have been with us this Christmas ... Our gallery was in great vogue, and really it is a charming room, for there are such variety of occupations in it, that people cannot be formal in it. Lord Harcourt was

writing, some of us played at whist, others at billiards, Mrs Gardiner at the harpsichord, others at work, others at chess, others reading, and supper at one end; all this without interruption to the different occupations. I have seldom seen twenty people in a room so easily disposed of.'

House parties in the country came with a presumption of greater informality than assemblies in town, and Louisa, with her increasing dislike of those she called 'fine men', consciously arranged her gatherings to insist upon it. Guests hunted, walked and drove about outside when the weather was good. They chatted, played cards, read aloud and picked up bits of 'work' like embroidery on long winter days and in the evenings. 'Mrs Walsingham, Mr

LEFT
A Castletown stable hand tempts a horse into being bridled with a handful of oats, in another of Healy's black and white paintings. Like the picture on the opposite page, this was painted as a summer picture, suggesting that Healy took some time to complete the whole set.

ABOVE

Healy's painting of the Castletown Hunt ready to set out across the countryside – a fine, unusual composition showing the early morning light seeping in on the left-hand side of the painting illuminating horses, rumps and dogs.

Coote, Lord Kerry, Mr Leeson, Lord Inchiquin, Mr Moore, Lord Powerscourt, Mr Conolly and I are all here now', Louisa reported to Sarah from Carton at Christmas in 1760. 'Yesterday morning there was a race between Mr Coote and Mr Conolly and another between Mr Moore and Mr Conolly. We went to see them, and to complete the day we acted in the evening "The Devil to Pay", none of us knowing any of our parts, which we had been studying all morning.' At this sort of party, wits like Emily's friends Lady Barrymore and Dean Marlay and Caroline's friend Frances Greville, and good-natured versifiers like Lord Russborough were coveted and valuable guests who helped while away Irish days of drizzle and fog.

Children, too, could make the time pass quickly. 'I was at Carton today', Louisa told Sarah in the spring of 1768, 'where the two youngest brats are. Gerald is a dear, beautiful child, and Augustus is in the Robert style, but not so large … Luckily for Cecilia and me he loves to be mumbled, and the more we kiss him, the more he laughs.'

Most aristocratic children spent their early lives in the country because it was regarded as more healthy than the town. City life usually began, for girls, with their coming out, and, for boys, with their beginning school. But there were some children, like the Foxes', who were metropolitan by education and instinct. The Foxes had no country estate when their children were young. Ste, Charles James and Harry Fox were Holland House children. Living on the edge of London they were spared its dust and smoke, but had the earliest possible exposure to its political and cultural life. Caroline encouraged their knowledge of the world and their precosity, the more so since Henry had neither title nor a great fortune when her children were small. She was determined that her sons should have success in the world of high politics in which she and Henry moved, and was convinced that starting young would set them on their way. All the Fox children learned to read and write early and to stay up late. Ste Fox knew the alphabet at eighteen months and, despite his constant illnesses, was an early reader. But it was Charles

RIGHT

Conolly in the last of Healy's series. Louisa was devoted to her racing, hunting squire of a husband. He loved her tenderly – but not faithfully – too. Others were less kind than she. 'I should never compare you to poor Conolly in anything', Emily told her husband, although she was the principal mover behind the marriage.

Frescati, Emily's school house, originally simply called Black Rock after the name of the village in which it was built; a photograph from the beginning of this century. Frescati was demolished after a long and ultimately fruitless campaign to save it, and a shopping centre now stands on the site. Emily's son Lord Edward Fitzgerald was as attached as she was to the house and its garden, calling it a kind of paradise, partly because it was his mother's house and partly because he thought her skill in planting and with flowers made it like the Garden of Eden.

who was brilliant. He was reading at two, devouring plays and novels by five and was marked out before he was seven as a future Lord Chancellor by his mother. Charles Fox grew up a lover of mathematics, of poetry, languages and history. Most surprising of all, he also grew up to be charming, lovable and much loved. Yet in spite of his precosity and early political success, Caroline did not relax; she expected even her grandchildren to be advanced and cultivated. Lord Holland, a famously indulgent father, was also an indulgent grandfather and enjoyed sending his granddaughter Caroline toys and trinkets. Caroline preferred presents that were rewards rather than playthings, as she told her son Ste in 1773. 'I am sorry Lord Holland would tell Caroline of the doll which may not arrive this month or two. Its bespoke at Paris and you know the arrival must be uncertain. To comfort her in the meantime I send her a little watch which I promised her when she could read and tell her I make no doubt that she can now she is past five years old.'

Sarah too, was ambitious for her five sons, born between 1781 and 1787, when she was between 36 and 43 years old. When she married George Napier against her brother's wishes, Sarah, like Caroline nearly forty years earlier – but to a much greater degree – was tossed out of the warm nest of Lennox connections and wealth. In time the Conollys offered Sarah and her family the sturdy cocoon of their income, but none the less, the Napiers' prospects and the prospects of their children were poor. Napier was always a falling rather than a rising star: a beautiful, intelligent, dissatisfied man; a career soldier who never rose above the rank of Colonel; a peer's son who came to espouse an ethic of duty to King and country that belonged more to the middling sort than the aristocracy of his day. Napier's sons, educated at the local school in Celbridge, would inherit nothing. Sarah was thus determined that they should not only make their own way, but should garnish the kind of plaudits that she felt their father had been unjustly denied. She encouraged her sons into the armed services for precisely this reason, as she explained to Susan O'Brien when they were poised to set off with General Moore on his Mediterranean expedition of 1805. 'I have made up my mind to my eldest three sons going with General Sir John Moore, because – what is their object in life? – fame, and where can they learn to deserve it better than in such a moment? A good cause, a good commander... and an early age when zeal is warm in their hearts and gilds every horror of war, leaving them only the duties of it to fulfil, which they long for.' Sarah's sons fulfilled her ambitions for them, although two of them, Charles James and William were frequently unhappy in their profession and came to feel as Charles James put it that 'war is licensed murder'.

By contrast, Emily, sitting in seeming security at the head of the Irish peerage, was lazy about her children's futures. Her children, in all their numbers, existed to adore her, to gleam and shine in little constellations at Carton and Black Rock as she turned the light of her maternal love upon them. Adore her they did; but in their early years they felt the warm light of her attention only intermittently. She was hardly out of childhood herself when she had her first child at the age of seventeen, and, growing up with her eldest children, she often left them in the nursery for weeks at a time while she went to Dublin or to London. In 1758 she happily dispatched eight-year-old George and seven-year-old William to London to go to school, consoling herself with the charms of her later arrivals, Emily, Henrietta, Charles and Charlotte.

Two things changed Emily's attitude towards her own motherhood and her children's education. The first was her reading of Rousseau's *Emile* or *de l'Education* of 1762. Caroline was the first of the Lennox sisters to read *Emile* and she used its tenets of late book learning and lessons from nature as much as her ambitions would allow in the education of her third son Harry. She sent the book to Emily, and followed by writing, 'You are in the Rousseau book I think now; I hope you like it. I am delighted with it and yet wonder how a book

ABOVE

Emily – Geraldine Somerville – and William Ogilvie – George Anton – at Black Rock in the early 1770s. Despite the fact that Ogilvie was a family servant, and at one time she had considered the necessity of his wearing uniform, Emily fell deeply in love with him, bowled over by his energy, his sexual power and his intense belief in himself.

ABOVE

William Ogilvie – George Anton – and Emily – Geraldine Somerville – with assorted Fitzgerald children on the beach at Black Rock. The Bray road inconveniently ran between the house and the sea, so a tunnel was dug to allow access.

setting out on a principle I think false, viz. the possibility of happiness in this world, so full of absurdities and paradoxes, can please me so much. Horace Walpole says its the finest piece of eloquence he ever read, and the first book that gave him an idea there was such a thing as French eloquence ... Several people say the first book is puerile and trifling – there, again, the vanity of our nature shows itself; we think ourselves

lowered by so much attention to our childhood.'

Emily was undoubtedly impressed by *Emile*. But it was not until the death in London of her eldest and favourite son George in 1765 that she actively espoused its principles. Overwhelmed by her son's death so far away from her, she determined never to send any of her children away to school again. Rousseau's scheme of country-based education with a tutor rather than learning with books and in boarding school now chimed with her wish to keep her children close by. The year after George's death saw the arrival of Rousseau himself in England. With characteristic extravagance Emily wrote offering 'an elegant retreat if he would educate her children'. At the same time she set about transforming the Duke's newly bought Black Rock villa into a Rousseauian school.

Rousseau declined Emily's invitation but the building went on. Early in 1768 William Ogilvie, a Dublin schoolmaster of obscure Scottish origins, was installed with Charles Fitzgerald and instructions for a modified Rousseauian curriculum. The experiment was such a success that the younger Fitzgerald children were one by one sent down to Black Rock. Emily began to live a triangular life, going to Leinster House for Dublin business and to lie in, to Carton for house parties and country air, and to Black Rock to see her children. She became an anxiously obsessive mother after George's death, demanding daily bulletins from Black Rock whenever she was unable to be there herself. More and more her world seemed to revolve exclusively around her family, as Louisa explained to Sarah in 1773. 'She says she loves children so much, that she shall desire no other company. Indeed I never saw anybody love children better than she does. She does dote upon little George Simon, who by the by, is such a favourite with us

all, that 'tis quite a shame. My sister owns that she loves him too much.' Louisa had failed to notice that wherever the Black Rock children were, William Ogilvie was too, and it was he as well as them who was the object of Emily's desire. Little George Simon died at the age of ten, and his death contributed to what Emily called in her old age 'the great misery and calamity of my life.'

ABOVE
Little Eddie – Lord Edward Fitzgerald's son, played by Owen O'Driscoll – follows Rousseau's prescription of close contact with the soil to the letter. The Fitzgerald children also dug the garden, sewed clothes and made hay in the meadow by the school house.

Travel

EMILY'S REFUSAL TO BE PARTED from her children meant that between 1765, when she took her son Charles to Malvern in Worcestershire, and 1774 when she came back because Caroline was dying, and then left to live in France, she did not travel out of Ireland. Of course she was not unusual in this rootedness; although the population of the British Isles was far more mobile than its continental counterparts, the vast majority of people did not travel abroad. Continental travel defined the traveller as wealthy and that, for the aristocracy, was one of its purposes. None the less, many aristocratic women did not travel much beyond a familiar round of London and the country, with a bit of sea-bathing in between. Emily's staying still was noticed partly because she had travelled to London quite often in the first few years of her marriage, and partly because she moved amongst people who were cosmopolitan and French-speaking, and who prided themselves on the breadth of their experience of man in many states and in many places.

It was a commonplace in the Lennox sisters' advanced Whig circle that travel was improving, intellectually, morally and even physically. It broadened the mind, thus making the traveller more understanding and even tolerant; it polished manners and it educated taste. It even, if French and Italian dancing and fencing masters were properly attended to, perfected deportment and bestowed an air of gentility and refinement on assiduous students. The British aristocracy were also enormously rich on the Continent, where in France and especially Italy it was possible to live in style much more cheaply than at home. Thus if travellers brought some sense of inferiority with them, partcularly in the areas of

ABOVE
Green ground Sèvres tea service, part of the collection made by the 3rd Duke of Richmond when he was ambassador in Paris in 1765–6. Caroline also bought a good deal of Sèvres for her private rooms at Holland House on her Parisian trips.

dress and deportment, where it was generally held that the French reigned supreme, they also brought bulging pockets with which they hoped to buy their way to refinement. Their riches gave them a kind of bravado, too, that enabled some travellers to despise as shallow the French and corrupt the Italians, while at the same time hoping that a bit of polish would rub off on them. Travelling, then, was a risky business, a process of garnering the good and avoiding the bad, a constant and sometimes anxious negotiation between the corrupting and the improving attractions of foreign places.

Extended continental travel was mainly a masculine affair. It was deemed unnecessary to 'finish' young women with any sort of travel,

and, once married, most aristocratic women were grounded by pregnancy and young children. Families did travel to take the waters in resorts like Spa in Belgium that were not too far from Britain, but not until the 1780s did families venture further afield in any numbers.

The Lennox sisters, however, had links with the Continent which predisposed them both to travel and to think of themselves as different from their contemporaries. Their great-grandmother was French, while their great-grandfather Charles II was half-French and had been brought up largely in France and the Netherlands. Louise de Kéroualle's château and the title of duc d'Aubigny had been passed down to her son and his heirs, and the sisters had never lost their attachment to France, their bilingualism and their belief in the superiority of French manners, literature and culture over English.

Caroline made her first trip to Paris in 1763 very soon after France was opened up again to British travellers at the end of the Seven Years War. Sure that she would find its inhabitants congenial, she was convinced that the city itself would be disagreeable. 'I was much determined against liking Paris', she told Emily, 'but I find I do; 'tis a pretty place indeed, full of fine hotels and large shady gardens to them, the streets so well paved and no black smoke in the town.' Sarah, who arrived a year later for the first of several visits that raised her spirits but contributed to the demolition of her marriage, agreed, writing to her friend Susan about Parisian apartments: 'They are mostly upon the ground floor and have every one a garden (where there are horse chestnuts for shade); the rooms are large, the windows immense and all down to the ground, the furniture very fine (if new), for there are commodes even in our lodgings, and looking glasses in every part of the room and very large ones. The houses are dirty and cold, but yet I own I like the style of them infinitely.'

The Lennox sisters' antecedents, the Ambassadorship of their brother to Paris in 1765–6 and Henry Fox's political contacts ensured that the Court and many aristocratic homes were open to them. Paris high society, like that of London, Vienna, Berlin and several Italian cities, prided itself on being cosmopolitan, and, besides, the *lingua franca* of the European aristocracy was French. The Foxes, and later Louisa and Sarah, went to Versailles, to the salon of Madame Geoffrin and the great houses of the anglophiles duc de Choiseul and Prince du Conti. Caroline's francophilia ensured

ABOVE

The anglophile duc de Choiseul, painted by Giovanni Paolo Pannini about 1757. The duc was host to many visiting English aristocrats, the Foxes among them. 'The French are the only people who understand all the ease of society', Caroline declared.

her a warm reception. 'I'm glad you hear the French people like me', she told Emily, 'because I really like many of them vastly. I like the turn of life and conversation there and their town of Paris most extremely.' Her 1763 stay was extended to seven months and she came back both in 1765 and 1766. Before she left the French capital in the spring of 1764, she summed up her liking for France and the French for her sister, saying, 'I do think they are the only people who know how to put society on an easy agreeable foot[ing]; they don't like to run after diversion, nor think themselves ennuyé unless there is something clever going on; they are trifling, chatty, and easy, have some formal old fashion'd customs which I was amazed at at first, but which clearly ... contribute to keep up a certain decency and politeness in society that we want. The men are not near so agreeable as ours, but a certain attention they pay to women of all ages makes up for the want of that superiority of understanding that our men are endowed with. The women in general are better than ours; every woman here has a character — the generality of ours have none. There is here a great attention paid to old people, and the old people here are exceedingly agreeable.'

In 1765 the Foxes party was enlarged not only by Louisa and Sarah, but also by Ste, Harry and Charles, the last removed from Oxford University and, at sixteen, said his proud mother,

'really extraordinary for his age; the complete student at Oxford, here quite the fine man, as much the coxcomb as is proper, and always in love, which I approve exceedingly'. Satirists were less indulgent when Charles James Fox arrived home; not only had he become debauched in Paris, it was said, but he came back with blue powder in his hair and red heels to his shoes.

But for young men, gaining sexual experience was part of the *raison d'être* – largely unspoken of course – of travel. The 'polish' that they gained on the Grand Tour was partly composed of

sexual confidence developed in the brothels and the drawing-rooms of the various European capitals through which they travelled. They would arrive home, the theory went, well versed in the language of love but not bringing a nurseryful of tiny mistakes with them. Foreign adventures came cheap and would not compromise British respectability, as Charles Fox himself recognized in a letter to a friend that he wrote from Florence during the family's extended journey of 1766–8. Fox went so far as to split his travelling self into two parts: while Charles

the English gentleman conversed in drawing-rooms, Carlo the raffish Italian went hunting pleasure on the streets. Carlo, he told a friend, had had a long wait, 'but in recompense for my sufferings I have now got the most excellent piece that can be allowed … There's a Mrs Holmes here, an Irish woman and more beautiful than words can express, and very agreeable into the bargain. Now it so happens that tho' this woman is exquisite entertainment for Charles, yet, as she is chaste as she is fair, she does not do for Carlino as well. There is also a silversmith's wife

ABOVE

The great palace of the Bourbon kings at Versailles. Caroline was gratified to be so pointedly noticed there. 'I went to chapel', she told Emily, 'saw the whole Royal Family coming from mass; in the antechamber the Queen and the Dauphin stopp'd to speak to me very graciously, which was very polite, as we English are not presented.'

Right

Lord William Fitzgerald, Marquis of Kildare and 2nd Duke of Leinster, painted with a book of maps as a young man. When he unexpectedly became his father's heir on the death of his older brother, his parents were in despair. 'Of all the difficulties I was ever under, what to do with William is the greatest I ever had', his father admitted. They shelved the problem by sending him on a very long Grand Tour, hoping he would come back polished and improved.

who is almost as fair as Mrs Holmes, but not near as chaste and she attracts me thither as regularly in the evening as the other does in the morning … This has led me to make verses and you shall soon have a poem of my own composing upon the pox in Latin.'

As Fox's letter shows, most grand tourists were very young. Before the idea of adolescence and at a time when the great universities' reputations were at such a low ebb that few aristocrats bothered sending their oldest children to them, the Grand Tour was a long, and for some, uncomfortable, rite of passage from youth to adulthood. Young men learned to head a household, take decisions, handle money (although most were accompanied by beady-eyed tutors), and complete their sexual, social and aesthetic education. The journey, which for some – like Charles James Fox, his friend Lord Carlisle and his cousin William Fitzgerald – might last three years, was thus a roundabout way of broadening the mind. It was a modern, secular pilgrimage on which grand tourists learned that life itself was a journey and adventure and that taking responsibility and learning to make judgements were processes of accumulating knowledge and making comparisons between different cultures, different peoples and different phases of history. 'After all we are but travellers in this world', Caroline reminded Emily before the whole Fox family set

off for Italy in 1766; grand tourists were supposed to learn that humbling truth and to come back with a true appreciation of man's achievements as well as God's works.

Many simply came back a little wiser and a lot poorer. For every Charles Fox – who had no need of a tutor, travelled with his family and learned Italian, perfected his French and versified in Latin – there was more than one William Fitzgerald, who went dutifully round Europe with a tutor, but still could write sadly from a boiling Florence in the summer of 1767, 'I own I shall be very glad when the time comes to return; I suppose in a year from this I may flatter myself.'

Caroline decided to make the long journey to Italy in 1766 partly to jolt her husband Henry out of the apathy into which he had sunk after his retirement from politics a year earlier and partly because she had for a long time harboured an ambition to see Rome and the sites she had read about in her history books. Besides their three sons and Ste's wife Lady Mary Fitzpatrick, the Foxes travelled with a full complement of servants including several maids, and Clotworthy Upton, an expert traveller and Italophile who had crossed the Alps ten times and was just the sort of companion Caroline needed, being, as she put it, a man of 'vivacity and good humour and a most violent, prejudiced Italian'.

ABOVE

The Santa Trinità Bridge in Florence, with the Ponte Vecchio behind it and an English Grand Tourist, Allen Smith, in the foreground, painted by François Fabre at the end of the eighteenth century. Although the Florentines had already established their reputation as closed and cold, their city and its environs were spoken of as unparalleled in beauty.

The whole party travelled slowly through France, with a generous stopover in Paris to satisfy Caroline's francophilia, and met William Fitzgerald at Lyons. William, who was shortly to become Marquis of Kildare when his father was elevated to the dukedom of Leinster, had already been in France for several months attending a military academy outside Paris. A gauche, plump, unremarkable young man, he had unexpectedly become heir to his father's title when his older brother died in 1765. All his life he was to labour in the dark shadow cast by his brother's

death and he never gained his mother's good opinion no matter how hard he tried. His aunt Caroline, who had looked after her sister's children in their Eton school holidays for almost a decade, was more indulgent, writing to Emily when the party had come together at Lyons, 'William is as dear, good a boy as ever lived, vastly obliging and attentive', and added, 'He goes every morning to the riding-house, which is I believe very good for him; he takes long walks and seems desirous of not growing fat.' There was indeed considerable pressure on young men to display a fine figure and William was much preoccupied with his portliness, so much so that one of his highest priorities on the tour was his shape. From Naples he sent his mother details of an expensive and sombre coat he had had made for the Birthday of the King, saying that the 'handsome velvet' 'becomes fat people best'. In Florence he was delighted to find that in the crippling summer heat he did not much want to eat, and that he would be 'thin as a whipping post before long, as he loses his appetite and does not sleep and sweats like a horse that has run a race.' In Rome he admitted to having kept a 'good table', but vowed that he wouldn't do it any more, and was finally able to claim a victory – undoubtedly temporary – in the battle with his shape and to write to his mother, 'I believe if you was to see me dance you would say the money was not lost.'

At Lyons the family party divided. William went with Henry and Charles James Fox down the Rhône to Marseilles and from there by boat to Genoa, Livorno and Naples. Caroline, Upton, Ste and Lady Mary and little Harry Fox all went overland, through Savoy, across Mount Cenis, down to Susa and Turin, and from there to Bologna and across the Appennines into Tuscany. Caroline was tired by the time the party reached Florence on 8 November, although she admitted that Mr Upton, 'has more spirits and good humour than anybody ever had, minds no

difficulties, bustles about and does everything for us.' Still, she told Emily, "Tis a most tedious and uncomfortable journey for a woman to make, and 'tho I meet with great amusement at times, it don't repay the trouble.' A week later, though, she had cheered up. It was people or 'mankind', as she put it, that she loved to observe as much as art and antiquities, and Florence offered plenty of opportunities for study and for her tartest commentary on them all. She went to the Uffizi galleries and was unmoved, finding that it 'answered my expectation, as all collections do – a very few fine things and a vast deal of tiresome stuff.' Calling on Sir Horace Mann, Britain's Minister at the Court of Tuscany for more than 45 years, gave her more fruitful material for her pen and allowed her to compare the Italians unfavourably with the French. 'I was at a conversazione at Sir Horace Mann's, an English assembly with the addition of a concert, only think how horrid! Lady Mary and I agreed we never saw such a set of vulgar stupid looking women; dressed up like our women of the town, showing such a quantity of neck, vastly laced up, no covering either on the head or neck, few of them talking anything but Italian, all with a man by her side, but no conversation seeming to pass between them … The way of life is unsociable to a degree. No people eat together; they live at the spectacle or these odious conversazione without any conversation together

except a man and a woman. ... Milan is the only town in Italy [where] people dine or sup together, and I own I'm so French as to think there is no society without it; you get more acquainted with people at table.'

Having fired off this satisfactorily sardonic broadside, Caroline was prepared to admit that the situation of the town was beautiful, writing, as generations of her fellow Englishmen and women would, 'the environs of it and the country about it are so enchanting they quite answer the most poetical descriptions. Orange

After 'four most fatiguing days' journey', Caroline's party arrived in Rome in mid-November. She was ready to be enchanted by the city's past, calling it, 'the heart of Empire, nurse of heroes and delight of Gods', but too eager to join Henry in Naples to stay for long. Reserving most of their pleasures – including that of having pretty Lady Mary sit to Pompeo Batoni – for the return journey, they set off after five days and were in Naples by the beginning of December. They found Henry Fox with Charles, William and Lord Carlisle already immersed in the rituals of grandtourism: visiting classical sites, climbing up Vesuvius (or, for less active visitors, watching its fiery glow at night), attending the Court of the young and boorish King, and going to the opera. Like his counterpart in Florence, the British envoy William Hamilton was indispensable to visitors and locals alike, becoming a man of influence by providing tourists with dancing masters and Italian teachers and introducing them to charlatans with 'restored' classical statues to sell as well as some dealers in genuine antiquities. Hamilton was in the perfect position of middle man and was enabled thereby to build up a fine collection of 'virtue' himself, although it was to be many years before he acquired his finest piece, the comely Emma, 2nd Lady Hamilton. 'He is a very civil and obliging man, and so is his wife', wrote the gullible William to his mother, adding,

LEFT
The Colosseum and the Arch of Constantine in Rome, painted by Canaletto. Caroline told Emily, 'I grow to like Rome very much; that is, the things that are to be seen there.' She was more critical of the people than their buildings, saying of the richer Italians that she met in Naples, 'there are many pretty looking women among them, some handsome, but all ordinary, noisy and underbred, debauch'd to a degree.'

groves, Catalonian jasmine hedges growing out in the gardens, and all the hills and sides of the hills cover'd with villas, cypresses, firs and the most beautiful buildings … I do wish you could see a villa by Florence. I'm quite wild about the air, the country and the prospects.'

BELOW
The Arch of Constantine, painted in the seventeenth century by Herman van Swanevelt. 'I love vastly to see places where such and such people have been, and where great events have happened', Caroline explained.

'they have been so obliging as to introduce Charles and I to almost all the first people here, who are very fond of the English'.

Everybody enjoyed themselves in Naples, watching the crowds of people in the streets, and going to classical sites. Caroline was pleased to be there and delighted to find Henry in such good spirits, telling Emily, 'I shall pass my time more agreeably here than in London, except the disagreeable idea of being so distant.' The teeming city seemed like a play staged for her pleasure. 'This town is excessively populous; there are numbers who live, I believe, in the street; one sees them settled there all day. The scene is odd and curious, the infinite variety of dresses pretty … the women have beautiful hair, and one sees it in full perfection, their great occupation being to louse one another in the streets all day long in the sun, and one sees such beautiful quantity of hair 'tis amazing. It is extremely entertaining to drive about the streets to see how very unlike everything is to what we see at home.' Caroline was also impressed with the ruins of Pompeii, though disappointed that no private houses had been excavated. 'We saw the remains of a small temple, of what is supposed to have been soldiers' barracks, a street, and one place supposed to have been a private house; but the simpletons throw the earth back again, and don't go on when they come to what they imagine was a private house, which is provoking, as one should have infinitely more curiosity to see that than any public building.' At the King's museum at Portici, too, Caroline's interest was caught by the domestic and by the striking similarity between modern and ancient artefacts. 'There is an entire set of kitchen furniture, very like our modern ones', she told Emily with obvious satisfaction.

The whole family, with William, his tutor Bolle, Clotworthy Upton and Charles Fox's friend Lord Carlisle, stayed in Naples until mid-March, when the party dispersed, Henry and Charles heading north by sea, William and Bolle

going to Rome overland, Caroline following him a few days afterwards with Upton, and Ste and Lady Mary Fox travelling with them before heading back to England via his old haunts in Switzerland.

Once she had turned north, Caroline felt she was on the way home, although she was to be still on the Continent – in Montauban and Nice – at the end of the year. At Rome she looked at more antiquities, attended the Easter rituals in St Peter's, and found time to visit other relics, the Young Pretender and his brother the Cardinal Duke of York. Bonnie Prince Charlie had been living out his days there in broken drunkenness since the débâcle of the Rebellion of 1745 ended at Culloden. Caroline delighted in her

own Stuart ancestry and enjoyed seeing her fellow descendants of Charles I, but their visits made William nervous, especially as the brothers were always closely watched by British spies who, although no longer interested in the brothers themselves, reported assiduously on their visitors. Caroline and Charles Fox, 'are most fearful J——', William reported to his mother, squeamish himself about about writing the word 'Jacobite'. He need not have worried though; Caroline's journey had made her utterly convinced of the evils of Catholicism and of war. From Protestant, bourgeois Switzerland on the last leg of her journey, she wrote praising the prosperity, rationality and peacefulness of the Swiss, and added, 'My travels, sweet siss, make me see the

BELOW

Rome seen by travellers, attributed to John Feary, 1780s. Caroline called it, 'the heart of Empire, nurse of heroes and delight of gods'.

misery caused by a superstitious religion and a great standing army in a light I never before saw it; to be sure priests and soldiers are the bane of human kind.'

After the Foxes' departure from Rome, William proceeded somewhat disconsolately to Florence. Although he kept meeting Old Etonians on his travels – 'I dare say I have met above forty since I have been in Italy' he wrote – he was, from now on, on his own. He was immediately lonely in Florence, partly because he arrived there in mid-June, just as most grand tourists and most grand Florentines were packing their bags to head north, in the case of the former, or outside the city to their country villas in the case of the latter. It was already intolerably hot, although, after some complaints and longing thoughts of the cool of Carton and the mists of an Irish summer, William determined to treat the heat in the way the locals did, sleeping,

'without a shirt and nothing but a sheet', and fanning himself in the evenings. 'It is the fashion here for men to carry fans, you know', he told his mother in July 1767. 'You know I like to be in the fashion, so I have got myself one, and when I dine at home I make use of it; and I also take it to bed and fan myself to sleep, which is very comfortable in this oven. But one meets the friars and all the gentlemen with them walking the streets of an evening.'

The problem of the Florentines was not so easily got over. They already had the reputation, which thrives to this day, of being cool and unsociable. 'I cannot say that the Florentines are the most agreeable people or the easiest to get acquainted with of any in Italy', he admitted, and went on, 'This seems an agreeable place enough, though I must own I am very much disappointed, as I expected to have found it a more beautiful place. It is astonishing the number of ugly women there are in this town, I can't find anything enchanting either in their person or their conversation to have conquered the hearts of so many English.' Something happened to make him change his mind, however, and sufficiently to alarm his parents that he was ordered in September to proceed to Turin and thence to Vienna. For the first time on

ABOVE
View of the Palazzo del Quirinale, Rome, by Michele Marieschi, about 1730. Caroline thought Rome would be disagreeable to live in. 'The pride and etiquette which is tiresome among all Italians is more here than anywhere, I understand', she told Emily.

The Ponte Molle, Rome, by Richard Wilson. Caroline liked driving about the streets and observing the 'common people', as she called them. RIGHT William Fitzgerald, painted by Sir Joshua Reynolds in 1775. 'William is so improved by his travel', wrote Louisa Conolly with relief when he finally came home.

his tour he protested, writing, 'I am much grieved at leaving Italy without seeing Genoa, Venice, Milan etc, etc. Also I left Florence very unwillingly, as I spent my time very well, having a great many acquaintances and talking the beautiful Tuscan language which, to be sure, is the most beautiful of all languages.' His parents suspected his pleasures were more amorous than linguistic and serious enough to warrant his removal. He was allowed to stay in Turin for several months, but then ordered on to German-speaking lands where his lessons would be military rather than social.

William was back in Ireland in the autumn of 1769. 'I fancy my time has not been lost by travelling', he said, and everyone agreed that he was much improved and matured by having been three years abroad. For two more decades young men followed his route and came back to a chorus of approval from their parents and relatives. After the French Revolution, however, the Grand Tour was suspended and afterwards most travel for young British men was to be imperial or military. Their close links with Europe were severed and henceforth British men would feel more at home in Bermuda than Bologna and more attracted by Delhi than by Dresden.

CHAPTER *5*

Endings

Elizabeth Armistead,
wife of Charles
James Fox, by Joshua
Reynolds. She was a
former courtesan who
had done the rounds of
Fox's circle before their
marriage. Fox remained
devoted to her. Seeing
her grief as he lay
dying, he murmured, 'It
don't signify, dearest,
dearest Liz'. She
cherished his memory
for another 40 years.

A TRANQUIL OLD AGE was unlikely to be the lot of those born in the first half of the eighteenth century and caught up in the great political dramas at its end: the French Revolution, the Irish rebellion and Union, and the Napoleonic Wars. Living as it had done for generations in the world of high politics, the Lennox family was closer than most to the turbulent epicentres, and relations within it were constantly shifting from the 1780s onwards as family members reacted in different ways to one great crisis or another.

Held together by the power and personality of Henry Fox, the family lost cohesion after he died in 1774. Ste Fox, who inherited the Holland earldom, was too infirm to have political interests or authority within the family. He died in 1775, leaving an infant son, and the Fox family mantle passed to his brother Charles James. By the early 1780s, Charles James Fox and his uncle the 3rd Duke of Richmond had fallen out both politically and personally. Fox's charisma, as well as his political beliefs, won over not only Emily and Sarah, but most of their children. Only Louisa remained loyal to her brother as head of the family.

When Charles James Fox went into Opposition in 1784, the 3rd Duke of Richmond remained in government, serving in Pitt's cabinet for most of the next two decades, as Master of the Ordnance. It followed that whereas the Duke followed the government line against the French Revolution, against independence for Ireland and in favour of war with France, the Foxites and their supporters in the Lennox family took the opposite view, both as a result of their political position and by conviction. The Duke's relations with

Goodwood House today, still the seat of the Dukes of Richmond. Essentially the work of the 3rd Duke and finished by his nephew, it still contains many fine portraits from the time of the 1st and 2nd Dukes.

Emily became distant, with Sarah downright stormy.

Sarah acknowledged her brother's good qualities but they never saw eye-to-eye after her marriage to George Napier in 1780. The Duke had hitherto served as trustee to her small fortune, and now she wanted her husband to play that role. Richmond refused and, so Sarah felt, underlined his opposition to her marriage by procuring Napier a wholly unsuitable and badly paid job in the Woolwich arsenal, when he could have made their lives easy with a far better sinecure. A quarrel ensued from which neither ever really backed down. Sarah remained an outspoken Foxite, fanatically opposed to William Pitt and his government, whom she blamed successively for the Irish rebellion, the Act of Union between Great Britain and Ireland and the long wars against France in which both her husband and her sons were caught up.

It was left to the next generation to patch things up. When Sarah's son Henry married the Duke's illegitimate daughter Caroline Bennett, 'the Lennox affection for one another', as Louisa called it, was reaffirmed. Sarah's children had quite a taste for family unions. William married Caroline Fox, daughter of Caroline's third son Harry – or General Henry Fox as he became.

Richard, Sarah's fourth son, married Anne Staples, a widow who had married into the Conolly family. Most surprisingly of all, her daughter Emily, adopted by Louisa and brought up at Castletown, eventually married Sir Henry Bunbury, nephew and heir to Sir Charles Bunbury, Sarah's first husband.

When the 3rd Duke of Richmond died in 1806, his title and estate, much encumbered by a debt of £180,000, went to his nephew Charles Lennox. The 4th Duke married Charlotte, heir to the last Duke of Gordon. It was a brilliant match which ensured the prosperity of the family by bringing with it the promise of the vast Gordon estates in Scotland when the Duke of Gordon died, as well as the Gordon name itself which was given life by grafting it on to the Lennox family, which after 1836 became Gordon-Lennox.

The family interests in France were less well protected. The Aubigny château, where Emily had lived between 1775 and 1780, was sequestered with the estate during the Revolution and turned into the Hôtel de Ville. Although the property was restored to the family in 1818, it was eventually broken up and sold to satisfy French inheritance laws in the 1840s.

Goodwood today is a thriving country estate, administered by the Goodwood Estate Company. Besides the park and house, the company runs the famous racecourse, the Goodwood Motor Circuit, a golf club, hotel and aerodrome, forest and farmland. The house itself, containing many fine portraits of the Lennox family, is rented out for functions and opened to the public in the summer.

Holland House, perhaps the most remarkable and unusual of all the Lennox family houses, did not share Goodwood's happy fate, although for many years it had a charmed existence while the 'great wen', as William Cobbett called London, grew around it. When Ste Fox died, his widow Lady Mary decided to let the house until her infant son Henry came of age. Putting aside only Caroline's magnificent portrait collection, she auctioned off the contents and turned the house over to tenants once more.

When the 3rd Lord Holland came into his inheritance, it was not his father's spirit, nor those of his grandparents, that came to dwell in Holland House's turrets and towers, but that of his uncle and mentor Charles James Fox. Fox had overseen Lord Holland's education; he treated his nephew as a son, affectionately called him 'young one', and passed him the mantle of Foxite opposition when he died in 1806. The 3rd Lord Holland was charged with keeping alive the Foxite flame, especially in the great questions of Catholic emancipation, abolition of slavery and peace with France. But he also inherited his uncle's love of literature, and Holland House, refurnished by his wife Elizabeth, became the

ABOVE
Goodwood estate servants in the mid-nineteenth century. RIGHT The 4th Duke of Richmond as a young man, painted by John Hoppner in 1790. Only son of Lord George Lennox, the querulous and difficult younger brother of the 3rd Duke, he knew by the time of this portrait that the title would be his.

foremost Whig salon in London, at which passing European politicians and exiles mingled with fashionable poets, and the Foxite legend was kept burning bright.

With the death of the 4th Lord Holland in 1878, the title became extinct, and Holland House passed into the family of the Earls of Ilchester, descended from Henry's brother Stephen and his child-bride Elizabeth Strangways Horner. The house continued to be the Fox-Strangways' London residence while the new suburbs of Notting Hill, Holland Park,

Kensington and Shepherd's Bush grew around it. In 1939, on the outbreak of war, the pictures in the house were taken to the Ilchester estate in the West Country for safe-keeping. Just over a year later Holland House was struck by an incendiary bomb and burned almost completely to the ground, leaving only fragments of the façade and part of the east wing – where Caroline had her private rooms, her greenhouse and her aviary – still standing. A Youth Hostel was constructed on the site; the ruin and grounds were turned over to Kensington &

ABOVE

Charles James Fox towards the end of his life, by Sir Thomas Lawrence. Edmund Burke called Fox 'a man made to be loved', and he was indeed adored, and shielded numerous times from bankruptcy by his devoted circle of friends and political associates. A man of generous and tranquil disposition, he said, hours before his death, 'I die happy', despite the fact that most of his political ambitions remained unrealized.

Chelsea Council and now form one of London's most intimate and best-loved parks. Caroline's paintings remain in the family house in Dorset, one of the most remarkable collections of English portraits in private hands today.

The Fitzgerald family houses survived better than its fortune. The rebellion of 1798 hit the family hard, both because of the prominent role of Lord Edward Fitzgerald and because their lands in County Kildare were largely laid waste. The Act of Union finished the political influence of Emily's son the 2nd Duke of Leinster and destroyed the family's political

power base by abolishing the Irish Parliament. Moreover the family had almost always been in political opposition both to Dublin Castle and to Westminster governments, so the Union removed their political role. The 2nd Duke had no Westminster base to move to, as did other politicians with Irish connections, like the Wellesleys and Lord Castlereagh. Union turned him simply into a private gentleman, and when he died in 1804, his heirs continued to fulfil that role, living out the nineteenth century as great landlords.

Leinster House in Dublin was sold in 1815, probably to discharge debts and pay for alterations at Carton. It became the home of the Dail after the founding of the Irish Free State, and although that necessitated the building of a debating chamber and many offices, it is, on the outside, still the imposing but dour mansion Emily disliked so much. Carton too, eventually passed out of family hands. Well-preserved but unlived in since the late 1970s, it is now owned by the Malagan family and formed one of the principal locations for the *Aristocrats* series. Frescati has had the most unhappy fate. It was demolished in the 1970s and a shopping centre built on the site.

When Louisa Conolly died, Castletown House passed to Colonel Edward Pakenham, a relative of Tom Conolly's. Colonel Pakenham changed his name to Conolly, and, although large

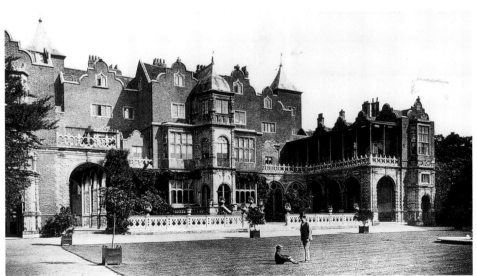

LEFT

Holland House at the beginning of this century and ABOVE on 23 October 1940 after it was firebombed. A few readers stand transfixed by the shelves of its famous library, despite the danger of imminent collapse. Only a shell remains today.

ABOVE
Carton House today from the air. It was used extensively to film the *Aristocrats* series. BELOW Castletown House today. At present under scaffolding, it could not be used for filming despite the fact that Louisa Conolly's gentle spirit still reigns supreme there.

parts of the family estates were sold off in the following century, the house stayed in the family until it was sold with 500 acres in 1965 to a Major Willson. Keeping back some of the land, Willson in turn sold it to Desmond Guinness two years later. This purchase saved Castletown for posterity. It was restored, and, administered by the Irish Georgian Society, gradually refurnished and opened to the public. Now in the hands of the Irish government, it is undergoing a major programme of renovation and will shortly reopen as a museum.

Although most of Louisa's furniture was removed from Castletown, her decorative schemes and her buildings in the park for the most part remain untouched. The long gallery,

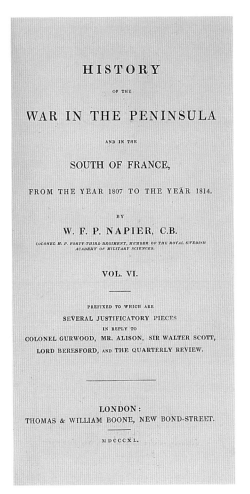

with its charming, idiosyncratic and slightly amateurish painted panels, is well preserved, and Louisa's print room, which is both unusually elaborate and a rare surviving example of a once-common decorative scheme, is in very good condition. More than any other of the surviving Lennox houses, Castletown retains the impress of a particular personality and manifests very strongly Louisa's own mixture of grandeur and informality.

After George Napier's death in 1804, Sarah wound up her Irish affairs and let the Celbridge house she had so happily built in the 1780s. It is now part of a school. Sarah moved to a London town house in Chelsea, staying in the same neighbourhood until her death in 1826. Her legacy was more in flesh and blood than bricks and mortar, her sons becoming heroic soldiers and famous Victorians. Charles James Napier – radical, difficult and a passionate philhellene – conquered the Indian province of Sind at the end of a long army career. He was carved in marble and winched by a grateful nation to the summit of a column in Trafalgar Square, slightly below the soaring eminence of the great Admiral Nelson. George Napier, too, became a successful general, Henry a sea captain and Richard a Fellow of All Souls and follower of John Stuart Mill. But it was Sarah's second son William, a man so handsome that he turned as many heads in the street as the prettiest of women, who had

the most remarkable career. After the peace in 1815 and a few desultory years on half-pay, he embarked on a monumental six-volume history of the Peninsular War, a work that can fairly said to have established a way of writing about war that is still in use a hundred and fifty years later in a thousand adventure stories, escape epics and tales of battle. But William Napier's transformation from soldier to historian was not surprising; all the Lennoxes were good writers, and William was every inch his story-telling mother's son.

ABOVE

Spine and title page of William Napier's *History of the War in the Peninsula*. Undertaken to defend the reputation of his beloved commander Sir John Moore, it established an heroic style of writing about war which has often been imitated but never surpassed.

Family Trees

The Lennox Family

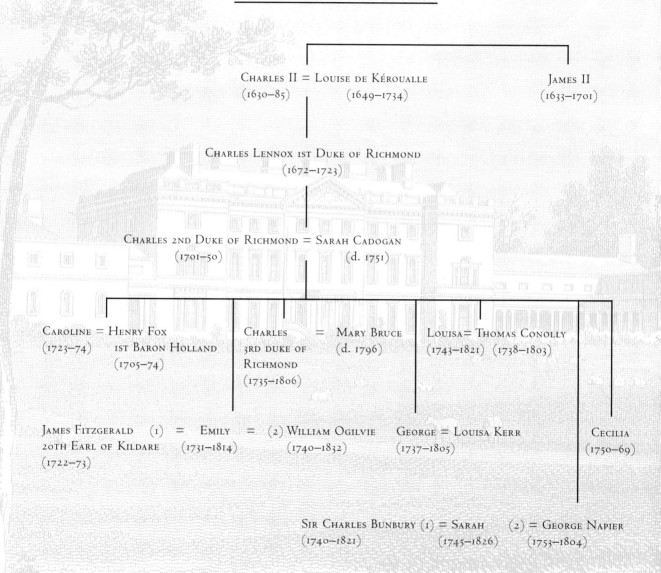

Charles II = Louise de Kéroualle   James II
(1630–85)   (1649–1734)   (1633–1701)

Charles Lennox 1st Duke of Richmond
(1672–1723)

Charles 2nd Duke of Richmond = Sarah Cadogan
(1701–50)   (d. 1751)

Caroline = Henry Fox   Charles = Mary Bruce   Louisa = Thomas Conolly
(1723–74) 1st Baron Holland 3rd duke of (d. 1796)   (1743–1821) (1738–1803)
      (1705–74)   Richmond
              (1735–1806)

James Fitzgerald (1) = Emily = (2) William Ogilvie George = Louisa Kerr   Cecilia
20th Earl of Kildare (1731–1814) (1740–1832) (1737–1805)   (1750–69)
(1722–73)

Sir Charles Bunbury (1) = Sarah   (2) = George Napier
(1740–1821)   (1745–1826) (1753–1804)

THE FOX FAMILY

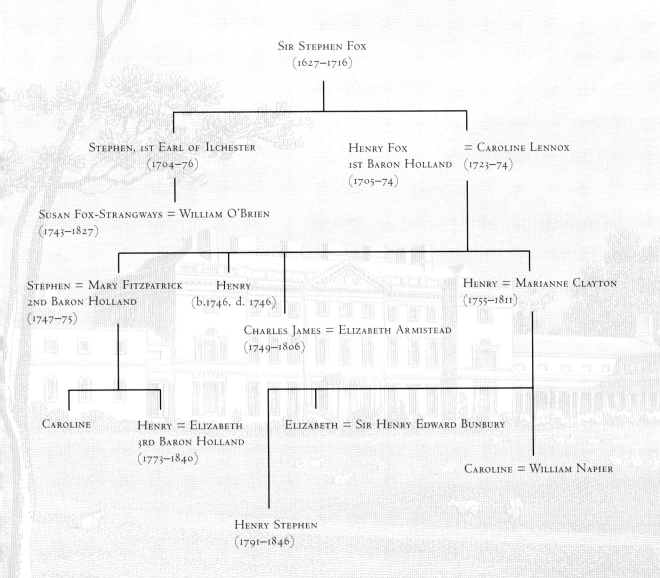

SIR STEPHEN FOX
(1627–1716)

STEPHEN, 1ST EARL OF ILCHESTER
(1704–76)

HENRY FOX
1ST BARON HOLLAND
(1705–74)
= CAROLINE LENNOX
(1723–74)

SUSAN FOX-STRANGWAYS = WILLIAM O'BRIEN
(1743–1827)

STEPHEN = MARY FITZPATRICK
2ND BARON HOLLAND
(1747–75)

HENRY
(b.1746, d. 1746)

CHARLES JAMES = ELIZABETH ARMISTEAD
(1749–1806)

HENRY = MARIANNE CLAYTON
(1755–1811)

CAROLINE

HENRY = ELIZABETH
3RD BARON HOLLAND
(1773–1840)

ELIZABETH = SIR HENRY EDWARD BUNBURY

CAROLINE = WILLIAM NAPIER

HENRY STEPHEN
(1791–1846)

The Fitzgerald and Ogilvie Families

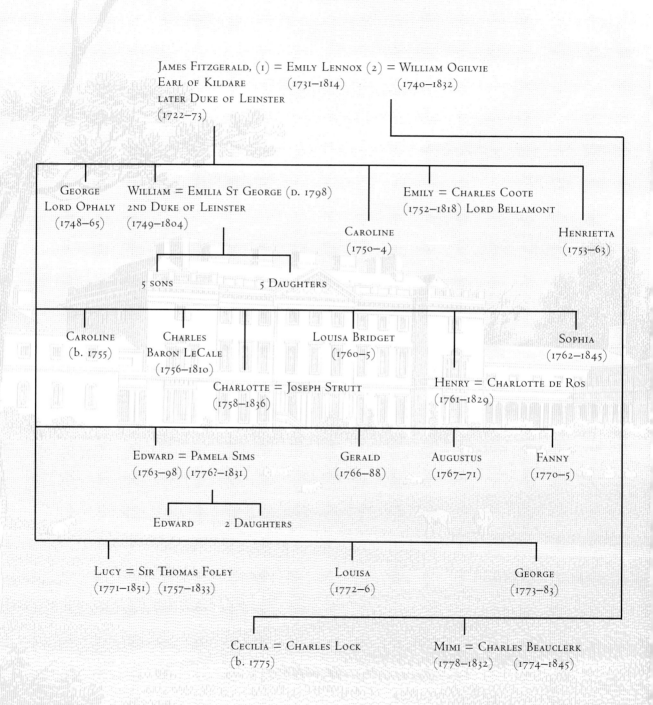

James Fitzgerald, (1) = Emily Lennox (2) = William Ogilvie
Earl of Kildare   (1731–1814)   (1740–1832)
later Duke of Leinster
(1722–73)

George
Lord Ophaly
(1748–65)

William = Emilia St George (d. 1798)
2nd Duke of Leinster
(1749–1804)

Emily = Charles Coote
(1752–1818) Lord Bellamont

Caroline
(1750–4)

Henrietta
(1753–63)

5 Sons   5 Daughters

Caroline
(b. 1755)

Charles
Baron LeCale
(1756–1810)

Charlotte = Joseph Strutt
(1758–1836)

Louisa Bridget
(1760–5)

Henry = Charlotte de Ros
(1761–1829)

Sophia
(1762–1845)

Edward = Pamela Sims
(1763–98) (1776?–1831)

Gerald
(1766–88)

Augustus
(1767–71)

Fanny
(1770–5)

Edward   2 Daughters

Lucy = Sir Thomas Foley
(1771–1851) (1757–1833)

Louisa
(1772–6)

George
(1773–83)

Cecilia = Charles Lock
(b. 1775)

Mimi = Charles Beauclerk
(1778–1832)   (1774–1845)

The Bunbury and Napier Families

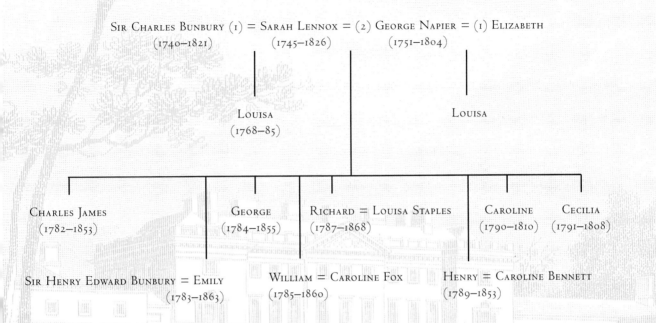

Sir Charles Bunbury (1) = Sarah Lennox = (2) George Napier = (1) Elizabeth
(1740–1821)   (1745–1826)   (1751–1804)

Louisa
(1768–85)

Louisa

Charles James
(1782–1853)

George
(1784–1855)

Richard = Louisa Staples
(1787–1868)

Caroline   Cecilia
(1790–1810)   (1791–1808)

Sir Henry Edward Bunbury = Emily
(1783–1863)

William = Caroline Fox
(1785–1860)

Henry = Caroline Bennett
(1789–1853)

Index

Art Directed by David Rowley
Designed by Nigel Soper
Edited by Anthony J. Lambert
Printed and Bound in Great Britain
by Butler & Tanner Ltd, Frome and London

Weidenfeld & Nicolson
The Orion Publishing Group Ltd
5 Upper St Martin's Lane
London WC2H 9EA

Acknowledgements

STELLA TILLYARD would like to thank all those at the BBC and Madikell
Limited who have helped in the production of this book, especially
Christopher Hall, who unflappably handled requests for names, times and
sundry other details; Derek Wax who kept house so well at Wood Lane;
James Keast, who answered my many questions about costumes and,
especially, stockings; David Caffrey, for his fun and Buddhist calm; James
Welland for his careful eye; David Snodin; Breda Walsh and Lisa Drayne.
Thanks, too – as usual – to Jenny Uglow and to Rosemary Baird and the
staff at the Goodwood Estate Office, and, at Weidenfeld to Michael Dover,
Caroline Knight, Anthony Lambert, Elizabeth Loving, David Rowley and
the inimitable Nigel Soper.

Picture Credits

(L=left; R=right; B=bottom)

©BBC: 4, 6, 7R, 8–10, 12R–15, 23–25, 57, 59, 76–79, 81, 92–105, 118, 121–122,
171–3. BRIDGEMAN ART LIBRARY: 19, 22, 51, 62; Scottish National Portrait
Gallery 87, 177, 178–9, Fitzwilliam Museum 182; Christie's 184–5;
Dulwich Picture Gallery 186, 188–190, 192, 197, 198. BRITISH LIBRARY: 114,
149, endpapers. CHRISTIE'S IMAGES: 28, 85, 88–91, 106, 113, 148. SYLVIA
CORDAIY: Roger Halls 54–5; Jonathan Smith 194. THE TRUSTEES OF
THE GOODWOOD ESTATE: 20–21, 26–27, 33–38, 46, 52–53, 58, 63, 66, 151,
176. HULTON GETTY: 29, 65, 199. IRISH ARCHITECTURAL ARCHIVE:
168–9. IRISH PICTURE LIBRARY: 72–75, 112, 120, 127, 128, 130–145, 147, 150,
153, 157, 200B. NATIONAL TRUST: Christopher Hurst 41; Andreas von
Einsiedel 70–71, 80–84. SYLVAINE POITAU: 2, 7, 11, 12, 17.

All other pictures are from private collections.

Cast List Caroline (19–45): Serena Gordon; Emily (17–40): Geraldine Somerville; Sarah (17–33): Jodhi May; Louisa (19–35):Anne-Marie Duff; Henry Fox (40–65): Alun Armstrong; Kildare (27–45): Ben Daniels; Duchess of Richmond (37–42): Diane Fletcher; Duke of Richmond (43–49): Julian Fellowes; Louisa (52): Diana Quick; Emily (64): Sian Phillips; Charles James Fox (15–25): Hugh Sachs; Edward Fitzgerald (30): John Light; Tom Conolly (22–35): Tom Mullon; Sarah (50): Sheila Ruskin; Charles, 3rd Duke (20–35): Tom Beard; Mary, Duchess of Richmond (20–35): Katherine Wogan; Ste Fox (17–27): Toby Jones; Ogilvie (52): David Gant; Pamela: Virgin Aster; Ogilvie (30–35): George Anton; Susan Fox Strangways (18–28): Pauline McLynn; Tom Conolly (54): Paul Ridley; Bunbury (22–25): Andrew Havill; Lord William Gordon (30): Gary Cady; George 2nd (61–65): Clive Swift; George Napier (47): Jeremy Bullock; George Napier (30): Martin Glyn Murray; Prince of Wales/George 3rd (21): Luke De Lacy

Unit List Director: David Caffrey; Producers: Christopher Hall, David Snodin; Executive Producer BBC: Michael Wearing; Writer: Harriet O'Carroll; Script Editor: Derek Wax; Production Manager: Seamus McInerney; Production Co-ordinator: Breda Walsh; Assistant Co-ordinator: Lisa Drayne; Production Accountant: John Mulligan; Location Manager: Dougal Cousins; 1st Assistant Director: Robert Quinn; 2nd Assistant Director: Suzanne Nicell; Casting Directors: John Hubbard, Roz Hubbard; Production Designer: Gerry Scott; Director of Photography: James Welland; Sound Recordist: Simon Willis; Make up/Hair Designer: Lesley Lamont-Fisher; Costume Designer: James Keast; Stills Photographer: Pat Redmond; Editor: Neil Thomson

Your Dear Brother one
he say'd going to Bou
parting and that see
wou'd not make up f
=ment and I believe
he always is, I am q
I know it will make
manner is so Sothin
=fort as well as pleasure
n very feeling one and
Ever my
Your b